A COMPANION GUIDE
TO THE SCOTTISH NATIONAL
PORTRAIT GALLERY

Michael
Gormley

0131 624
6314

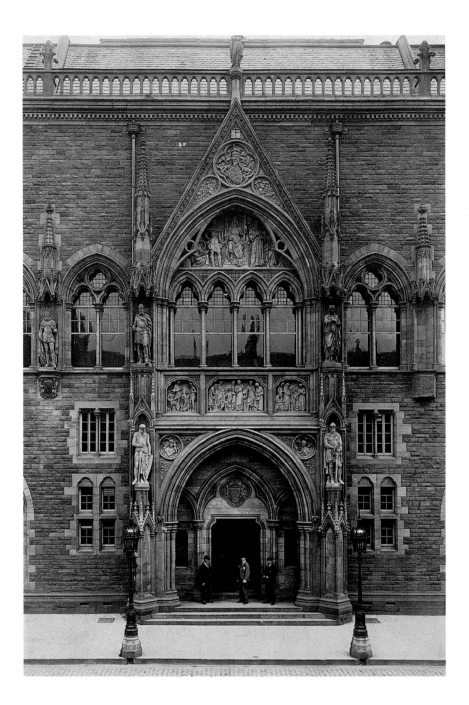

A Companion Guide to the Scottish National Portrait Gallery

NATIONAL GALLERIES OF SCOTLAND
EDINBURGH · 1999

Published 1999 by the Trustees
of the National Galleries of Scotland

© The Trustees of the National Galleries of Scotland
ISBN 0 903598 70 1

Designed and typeset in FF Quadraat by Dalrymple
Printed in China by Toppan Printing Company
(Shenzhen Limited)

Foreword

In recent years the National Galleries of Scotland have become increasingly active in organising major loan exhibitions, yet we have been equally active in expanding our permanent collections and making them better known. Besides making many outstanding additions to our collections we have also published concise, illustrated catalogues of the works belonging to the Scottish National Gallery of Modern Art, Scottish National Portrait Gallery and National Gallery of Scotland. This fully-illustrated *Companion Guide* to the Portrait Gallery marks another step towards enhancing public awareness of our remarkable collections. A second volume on the Gallery of Modern Art is also available, and a third volume on the National Gallery collection is in preparation. Lavishly illustrated, informative and reasonably priced, these books will, we trust, allow more and more people to share in the enjoyment of our collections, and encourage more and more to visit the National Galleries of Scotland.

TIMOTHY CLIFFORD
Director, National Galleries of Scotland

Thomas Carlyle by Helen Allingham, 1879
Watercolour, 19.4 × 28
Bought in 1915
PG 845

Introduction

The Scottish National Portrait Gallery, as its name implies, houses Scotland's collection of national portraits. It is a huge collection, numbering tens of thousands of images. This *Companion Guide* can only skim the surface yet it is the fullest ever published and is, in itself, an important visual record of Scottish history and achievement.

Scotland has produced an astonishingly high number of men and women whose lives have inspired and changed the world. In the fields of science, medicine and philosophy, in literature and the visual arts; in military affairs, the church and in sport, Scots have shaped the very way we live and think. Perhaps no country of similar size has contributed so much.

The sometimes turbulent and romantic history of the country is recalled in this guide by the portraits of Mary, Queen of Scots and John Knox, of Montrose and Bonnie Dundee, of Prince Charles Edward Stewart and Flora Macdonald. Here too are scientists of genius: Joseph Black and Lord Kelvin, for example, the great philosopher, David Hume, the architects Robert Adam and Charles Rennie Mackintosh – men and women whose fame transcends national boundaries. The lives of all of us today, Scots or not, would be unimaginable without the invention of the steam engine or television, our health in danger without anaesthetic or penicillin, our imagination duller without Dr Jekyll and Mr Hyde or Peter Pan – all these, and many more, are the products of Scottish genius; their creators illustrated in this guide.

The origins of the Scottish National Portrait Gallery can be traced back to the late eighteenth century and to the enthusiasm of one man, the mildly eccentric, David, 11th Earl of Buchan. He started to collect portraits for a Temple of Caledonian Fame and chose the Chapter House at Dryburgh Abbey to house them. Lord Buchan's Temple did not outlast the man, but much of his collection survives and forms the foundation collection of the Scottish National Portrait Gallery.

The Portrait Gallery, which opened its doors to the public in 1889, owed much as well to the inspiration of the historian Thomas Carlyle. A believer in heroes, Carlyle held strong views on the importance of portrait collections. 'It has always struck me', he wrote in support of Scotland's campaign for a National Portrait Gallery, 'that Historical Portrait Galleries far transcend in worth all other kinds of National Collections of Pictures whatever; that in fact they ought to exist ... in every country, as among the most popular and cherished national possessions.'

His sentiments were widely shared although the government of the day refused, initially, to commit public funds. It took the philanthropy of a local newspaper proprietor, John Ritchie Findlay, to pay for the building and create an endowment. Anonymous for as long as it was possible, Findlay masterminded the construction of the remarkable building which houses the collection. Sir Robert Rowand Anderson was Findlay's architect and he went to great lengths to create a modern purpose-designed art gallery equal to the most advanced at that date in Europe or America. At the same time, Rowand Anderson wanted his building to be a shrine for Scotland's national portraits and he planned the extensive decorative scheme both external and internal, to be essential components of the visitor's experience. The sculptural programme on the north and west facades were the most important sculptural commissions of the nineteenth

MOORE JEFFREY SCOTT BURNS TELFORD BRUCE DUNCAN CULLEN SMITH FORBES GE
OCH RAEBURN HUNTER HUTTON WATT ADAM BOSWELL ROBERTSON HUME MUR

8

LORA CDONALD CH:EDWARD LOCHIEL RAMSAY THOMSON MAR FLETCHER ARGYLL STAIR DUNDEE JAMES VII LAUDER DALE CHARLES II LEIGHTON MONTROSE ARGYLL LESLIE JAMESON CHARLES I OTHI

Above: the east wall of William Hole's pageant frieze, charting Scottish history from 1649 to 1801.

Opposite: St Columba's Mission to the Picts, 1898, one of the murals by William Hole on the ambulatory around the main hall.

century. Poets, monarchs and statesmen keep watch over Queen Street and North St Andrew Street while William Wallace and Robert the Bruce guard the entrance.

In the dramatic and atmospheric main hall, William Hole's pageant frieze provides the visitor with a convenient aide-memoire to Scottish history. Above, also by Hole, are murals depicting battles for Scottish independence and other historic events too early in date to have been recorded by native artists. Portrait painting came late to Scotland. Not until the last decades of the sixteenth century do there appear to have been artists of quality resident in the country. The murals, the frieze and the external sculptures are particularly important in helping to recall, albeit imaginatively, the early chapters of Scottish history; the latter of which are told by the national portrait collection itself.

For the first one hundred years of its existence the Gallery shared its building with a number of learned societies the last of which, the Society of Antiquaries of Scotland and its museum, is finally leaving for a permanent home elsewhere.

The expansion of the Portrait Gallery to embrace the whole of the building designed for it will take place over several years when the opportunity will also be taken to install those services and facilities which it has long lacked.

Portraits have always been made in a wide variety of media. This *Companion Guide* reflects that diversity and includes medals, engravings, silhouettes and photographs as well as oils, drawings and sculpture.

The criterion for inclusion in the collection is, first and foremost, the importance of the sitter. The rule of thumb is that entry is reserved to those said to have made a distinctive contribution to Scottish life. Generally, that contribution is a positive one, but there are a few men and women in the collection whose dishonourable behaviour have earned them their place. Burke and Hare, the two most notorious criminals of the nineteenth century, are in this Guide. So too is the disreputable Lord Lovat – in a memorable portrait by Hogarth.

Recently, the remit of the Gallery has been widened to allow it to collect masterpieces of Scottish portraiture, regardless of the prominence of the individual. Portraits illustrated in this guide which have been bought on that

9

Sir Robert Rowand Anderson 1834–1921,
the architect of the Gallery
Design for the commemorative window
by W. Graham Boss

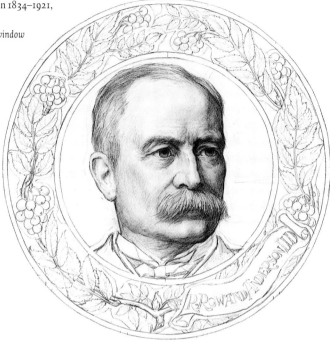

John Ritchie Findlay 1824–1898,
the founder and principal benefactor
of the Gallery
Design for the commemorative window
by W. Graham Boss

The Scottish National Portrait Gallery, drawn by Thomas Crawford Hamilton in 1890.

account include John Michael Wright's *Countess of Cassillis* and Allan Ramsay's *Anne Bayne*.

Unlike its sister galleries, the National Gallery of Scotland and the Scottish National Gallery of Modern Art, the Portrait Gallery is willing to acquire and display works of inferior quality providing, of course, that the sitter is important. This Guide includes a few such portraits. Happily, their number is outweighed by many great masterpieces – paintings and sculptures which would not be out of place in the most illustrious art galleries in the world. This Guide illustrates many of the greatest of them: paintings by Van Dyck and Gainsborough, by Ramsay and Batoni and sculptures by Chantrey and Thorvaldsen.

The Gallery continues to collect, both to add portraits of those men and women missing from the collection – the engineer Thomas Telford, the physicist James Clerk Maxwell and the writer Edwin Muir are much lamented absentees – and to bring the collection up-to-date. Since 1982 there has been a policy of commissioning portraits of living Scots by imaginative and innovative artists. Avigdor Arikha's portrait of the Queen Mother was the first such commission. Several others are included in this Guide.

The money to run the Gallery and acquire works comes from the government via the Scottish Office. Funds for acquisitions have been generously supplemented by donations from the National Heritage Memorial Fund, the Heritage Lottery Fund and, over many decades, the National Art Collections Fund. Looking through this Guide, written and produced by all members of the Gallery's curatorial staff, the reader will quickly appreciate the great and continuing generosity of individuals. Without their support Scotland's national portrait collection could never have developed into the comprehensive national collection it can proudly claim to be.

JAMES HOLLOWAY
Keeper, Scottish National Portrait Gallery

Mary of Guise 1515–1560 by *Corneille de Lyon*

Oil on panel, 22 × 15.1
Gifted by E.P. Jones in 1950
PG 1558

Mary of Guise is best known as the mother of Mary, Queen of Scots. The eldest daughter of the powerful Claud, Duke of Guise, she was first married to the Grand Chamberlain of France, Louis, Duke of Longueville. He died young, leaving her pregnant, and with a young son. She would have preferred to remain in France, looking after her children's interests, but the French king decided that she should marry James V of Scotland.

At first, things went well. Very tall, healthy and strong, Mary had two more sons by James V, but shortly after the birth of the second, they both died, within hours of each other, and in the late autumn of 1542 James's army was defeated by the English at Solway Moss. He sank into a deep depression and died a few days after Mary had given birth to their daughter, who now became Mary, Queen of Scots. By her marriage contract Mary of Guise was free to return home to France but she stayed on in Scotland, trying to protect her daughter's interests. For a time she ruled as Regent, struggling to keep the country in the French Roman Catholic interest and trying in vain to stem the rising tide of Protestantism. She died in Edinburgh Castle in June 1560.

John Knox c.1512–1572 from Theodore Beza's Icones, after Adrian Vanson

John Knox, a native of Haddington, began his career as a Roman Catholic priest, but by 1546 he had become an enthusiastic supporter of the Protestant preacher, George Wishart. Captured by the French when they took St Andrews Castle and sent to the galleys, he later made his way to Protestant England, where he gained a reputation as an energetic preacher, and was offered the bishopric of Rochester, which he declined.

When Mary Tudor inherited the English throne, he took refuge on the Continent, first at Frankfurt, then in Geneva, becoming a great admirer of John Calvin. He visited Scotland in 1556, returning permanently in 1559. His sermon at Perth on idolatry led to riots against the Roman Catholic Church, and he vigorously condemned the Mass when Mary, Queen of Scots returned to her realm in 1561, having several famous confrontations with her. By that time he was minister of St Giles, in Edinburgh, a position he held until his death. There has been some argument as to whether this engraving is an authentic likeness of him, but there is strong evidence to accept it as his portrait. It has been used as the basis for various statues and history paintings.

Wood engraving, 13 × 10
Published in 1580
Bequeathed by W.F.
Watson in 1886
PGE 27

IOANNES CNOXVS.

George Buchanan 1506–1582 attributed to Arnold Bronckorst

George Buchanan's fame in his own day rested on his international reputation as a classical scholar, but he has been best known ever since as one of the leading accusers of Mary, Queen of Scots.

Born at Killearn, in Stirlingshire, in 1506, he was educated at the universities of Paris and St Andrews, and had a distinguished career teaching in the universities of France and Portugal. He was for a time tutor to an illegitimate son of James V, and, on the return to Scotland of Mary, Queen of Scots in 1561, he was high in her favour, often reading Livy with her in the evenings. He turned against her, however, after the murder of Lord Darnley, publishing a vehement denunciation accusing her of luring her husband to his death and he helped to prepare the case against her at her trial in York. As tutor to James VI, he not only gave the boy a rigorous academic education, but did everything he could to turn him against his mother.

This portrait was painted the year before his death, when he was completing his history of Scotland, *Rerum Scoticarum Historia*. The inscription reads (in translation): 'So were Buchanan's features and countenance. Seek his writings and the stars if you wish to know his mind.'

Oil on panel, 34.1 × 27.7
Dated 1581
Bought in 1985
PG 2678

Mary, Queen of Scots 1542–1587

Den VIII february werde onthalst Maria
Stuart Schots Coninginne s terwende roomsch Catho-
lyck Hebbende gesocht veel onrust ten aen te richten Haer selven
mee ter te maecken van Engelant t dwelck Haer vanden tract
ofte parlement volcomelyck werde vertoont, Anno 1587.
Metren XIII fol XIII en XIIII b

The Execution
of Mary, Queen of Scots
by an unknown artist
Watercolour on paper,
21.9 × 26.4
Bought in 1934
PG 1217

Mary, Queen of Scots, one of the most romantic figures in Scottish history, ended her life on the scaffold of Fotheringhay Castle, near Northampton, on 8 February 1587. After nineteen years in captivity in England, she had been tried and condemned to death for plotting the assassination of Queen Elizabeth I. The full-length portrait of her, an early seventeenth-century copy, derives from the time of her captivity, while the watercolour records in detail the events of her execution. The earls of Kent and Shrewsbury are seated to the right, the Dean of Peterborough in the foreground exhorts her to repent, and her physician, steward and two men servants kneel at her feet. Her two favourite women attendants, Jane Kennedy and Elizabeth Curle, stand weeping to one side of the scaffold while the executioner raises his axe.

Afterwards, Mary's clothes were burned, to prevent her supporters from keeping them as relics, and this is the scene visible on the far left. The houses in the background and indeed the costume of the participants are distinctly Dutch, a fact not altogether surprising since this drawing seens to have been specially done for an album of historical prints and drawings compiled by Willem Luytsz. van Kittensteyn, a Delft magistrate, in 1613.

MARIA
D G
SCOTIÆ
PIISSIMA REGINA
FRANCIÆ DOTARIA
ANNO
ÆTATIS REGNIQ
36
ANGLICÆ CAPTIVIT
10
S H
1578

Henry Stewart, Lord Darnley 1545–1567 by Hans Eworth

Oil on panel, 70.4 × 55.2
Dated 1555
Bought in 1980
PG 2471

Lord Darnley's father, the Earl of Lennox, one of Scotland's leading noblemen, was the descendant of James II of Scotland, while his mother, Lady Margaret Douglas, was a granddaughter of Henry VII of England. Darnley was brought up at Temple Newsam, near Leeds. Conscious of her son's dynastic importance, Lady Lennox had him carefully educated in all the courtly accomplishments. This picture was painted in 1555, when he was ten, presumably during one of the family visits to London. He is dressed in the height of fashion, his dark doublet trimmed with gold aglets and a sword worn at his waist.

He met his cousin Mary, Queen of Scots briefly on two occasions, when his mother sent him over to France in 1559 and again in 1561. Four years later, he travelled to Scotland and met Mary for a third time at Wemyss Castle in Fife. She was a widow now and, encouraged by his mother, she married him. Their only child, James VI, was born in 1566. The following year, Darnley was murdered at Kirk o'Field, the Edinburgh house where he had been recuperating from smallpox.

James Hepburn, 4th Earl of Bothwell c.1535–1578 and Lady Jean Gordon, Countess of Bothwell 1544–1629 by an unknown artist

After the death of Lord Darnley, at Kirk o'Field, Mary, Queen of Scots ignored the advice of her friends and married James, 4th Earl of Bothwell, the man generally believed to have been responsible for the murder. About seven years older than she was, Bothwell had been a loyal supporter of her mother. In 1566 his financial difficulties had caused him to marry Lady Jean Gordon, the wealthy sister of the Earl of Huntly. These tiny paintings date from the year of their wedding and show him in a high-necked yellow doublet, his wife in fashionable black, with gold chains and a French hood.

He was by then a close friend of the queen, and in April 1567 he abducted her, probably with her consent. He had his marriage annulled and on 15 May he and Mary were married at Holyroodhouse in a Protestant ceremony. He was with her when she was confronted at Carberry Hill by her Protestant lords. She eventually surrendered to them while he rode away to seek help. They never saw each other again. He was arrested in Norway and spent the last eleven years of his life in prison. Lady Jean married twice more, living to the age of eighty-five.

Oil on copper,
3.7 and 3.5 diameter
Both dated 1566
Bought in 1917
PG 869 & PG 870

James Douglas, 4th Earl of Morton c.1516–1581 by Arnold Bronckorst

Oil on canvas,
106.3 × 82.1
Bought in 1959
PG 1857

James, 4th Earl of Morton, was involved in all the most dramatic events of the reign of Mary, Queen of Scots. A leading Protestant, he became her Lord Chancellor in 1563. He was one of those who burst into her supper chamber three years later and murdered her secretary, David Riccio, and he was implicated in the murder of her second husband, Lord Darnley. He was at Carberry Hill when Mary surrendered to her Protestant lords, led the vanguard at the battle of Langside and conveniently 'discovered' the mysterious Casket Letters, now believed to be forgeries, which seemed to prove that she had lured Darnley to his death. Morton ruled Scotland from 1572 to 1578 during the minority of James VI, working hard to maintain friendship with England and dealing ruthlessly with Mary's supporters. This portrait, showing him in fashionable black doublet and sugar-loaf hat, was painted about 1578. The castle in the background is perhaps a fanciful representation of Aberdour or Tantallon. Two years later his enemies denouced him as one of the murderers of Lord Darnley, and in June 1581 he was executed on the Maiden, the guillotine which he himself had introduced into Scotland.

Lady Agnes Douglas, Countess of Argyll c.1574–1607
attributed to Adrian Vanson

Oil on canvas, 86.4 × 77.5
Dated 1599
Bequeathed by the Marquess
of Lothian in 1941
PG 1409

Lady Agnes and her six sisters, daughters of the 6th Earl of Morton, were known for their beauty as 'the seven pearls of Lochleven'. When this portrait was painted in 1599 Lady Agnes was twenty-five and had been married for seven years. Her husband was the Earl of Argyll, an important soldier and statesman, recently created a privy councillor.

Lady Agnes's red hair is swept up and padded into a heart-shaped arrangement outlined by an attire of seed pearls. All her jewellery looks forward to seventeenth-century fashions, the settings more delicate than in the previous century but nonetheless drawing attention to the wealth of the beautiful young countess.

James VI and I 1566–1625

James VI was the only child of Mary, Queen of Scots and her second husband, Lord Darnley. This beautiful miniature shows him in winged doublet and lace-edged standing collar, the badge of the Order of the Garter round his neck. By the time it was painted, he had inherited the throne of England from Elizabeth I, having ruled Scotland shrewdly and successfully for many years. He had still been a baby when he was crowned King of Scots after his mother's forced abdication in 1567, and his troubled childhood, disturbed by the machinations of the ambitious nobility, made him all the more delighted to move south in 1603 to London, where his prestige as well as his personal security were greatly increased.

He liked to boast that he thereafter ruled Scotland with the stroke of his pen, and indeed his knowledge of his own countrymen allowed him to govern effectively from more than four hundred miles away. Scotland retained its own parliament and legal system, but James did what he could to encourage a more complete union of his two kingdoms.

Lady Arabella Stuart c.1577–1615 attributed to Robert Peake

Arabella was the only daughter of Lord Darnley's younger brother, Charles, and a first cousin of King James VI. This picture's traditional identification as Arabella is borne out by its similarity in features to the only certain portrait of her, a full-length at Hardwick Hall, Derbyshire. Here, she wears a black dress with a large ruff. On her left wrist perches a little pet dog, and in her right hand she holds an open watch, that customary reminder of mortality. The inside of the watch lid has the date 1605 inscribed upon it.

Arabella was brought up in England, and because she was closely related to the king, she was the centre of plotting and intrigue. A clever, difficult, headstrong girl, she was at first treated kindly by James VI and I, but in 1610 she secretly married William Seymour, who also had a claim to the throne of England. Believing that she had a sinister purpose for the marriage, James had her imprisoned in the Tower of London. Probably the following year, a silver medal was produced on her behalf, bearing her image on one side and the words, 'In that I suffer wrong, O God grant patience'. She never was released, and she died in the Tower in 1615.

Oil on panel, 90.2 × 70.4
Dated 1605
Bought in 1884
PG 9

Elizabeth, Queen of Bohemia 1596–1662
from the studio of Michiel van Miereveld

Oil on panel, 66 × 55.9
Gifted by Arthur W. Brown
in 1917
PG 1053

Elizabeth Stewart was the daughter of James VI and named after her god-mother, Queen Elizabeth I of England. She was brought up at Linlithgow Palace but moved south with her family when her father succeeded Elizabeth to the throne of England. Very eligible, as the king's only daughter, she married a German prince, Frederick V, the Elector Palatine.

The young couple settled happily in Heidelberg. Their lives changed dramatically in 1619 when the Protestants of Bohemia chose Calvinist Frederick as their king. Frederick and Elizabeth were aware of the perils of accepting the throne of a state entirely surrounded by hostile Catholic

neighbours. From the start, their enemies called them the Winter King and Queen, predicting, accurately, that their sovereignty would be brief. Frederick was defeated at the battle of the White Mountain and the royal couple were forced to flee Prague.

Frederick spent the remainder of his short life vainly trying to regain his own lands which had also been captured by the Catholic imperial army. He died in 1632. Elizabeth lived on, in exile in The Hague. Her debts mounted and her brother, Charles I, was executed in England. She lived long enough, however, to see her nephew, Charles II, restored to the British throne and in 1661 she returned to London.

James, 3rd Marquis and 1st Duke of Hamilton 1606–1649 by Daniel Mytens

Oil on canvas, 221 × 139.7
Dated 1629
Bought with help from the National Art
Collections Fund, the National Heritage Memorial
Fund and the Pilgrim Trust in 1987
PG 2722

James, Duke of Hamilton, was the close friend and principal Scottish adviser of Charles I. This picture was painted when he was twenty-three, by Daniel Mytens, and it is one of the finest portraits of the period. The following year, Charles I sent Hamilton to Germany with a force to fight in the Protestant armies of Gustavus Adolphus, but the expedition was not particularly successful and he soon returned to London.

When the king's ecclesiastical policies led to trouble in Scotland, Charles sent him north as commissioner to the Glasgow General Assembly of the Church of Scotland in 1638, but the situation was by then beyond repair. In the turmoil of the Civil War he was a moderate, advising caution, while his rival the Marquis of Montrose proposed more daring solutions. The king began to doubt his loyalty and imprisoned him in Pendennis Castle. Released when the castle was captured by the Parliamentarians, he led the 1648 expedition which attempted to rescue Charles. Defeated at the battle of Preston and captured soon afterwards, he was tried for treason and executed less than six weeks after the king, on the same scaffold at Whitehall.

Alexander Henderson c.1583–1646 by Sir Anthony van Dyck

Alexander Henderson was one of the most important figures in the Church of Scotland in the early seventeenth century. Born at Creich, in Fife, he was educated at the University of St Andrews and became Professor of Rhetoric and Philosophy there, before becoming successively minister of Leuchars and then St Giles in Edinburgh, John Knox's former church.

Henderson opposed James VI's ecclesiastical policies, particularly the Five Articles of Perth, and led the opposition to the prayer book which Charles I was determined to impose upon the Scottish church. One of the authors of the National Covenant, he was moderator of the famous 1638 Glasgow General Assembly which challenged royal policies. He entered England with the Covenanting army in 1640.

Despite this, Charles I, who had a high regard for his piety, made him his chaplain during his visit to Scotland in the autumn of 1641. Later, when he was with the king at Oxford, he urged him to call a Scottish parliament. He drafted the Solemn League and Covenant in 1643, later corresponding with the king about episcopacy and his coronation oath. This austere portrait of him, by Charles's court painter, Van Dyck, probably dates from 1641, when Henderson was in London negotiating with the king.

Oil on canvas, 127 × 105.4
Bought with help from the
National Art Collections
Fund and the Pilgrim Trust
in 1974
PG 2227

King Charles I 1600–1649

The Execution of
Charles I
by an unknown artist
Oil on canvas,
163.2 × 296.8
On loan from Lord
Dalmeny
PGL 208

On 30 January 1649, Charles I walked for the last time into his Banqueting House at Whitehall. The shy child of Robert Peake's early portrait had grown into a stubborn man whose ecclesiastical and fiscal policies plunged Britain into civil war and had ended in his defeat and imprisonment. Charles had been tried by the Cromwellians, found guilty and sentenced to death. He put on two shirts that morning, so that people would not see him shiver with cold and think that he was afraid. It was two o'clock in the afternoon when he stepped from a window on to the black-draped scaffold outside. Taking off his Order of the Garter, he put on a satin cap and then placed his neck on the block. The masked executioner stepped forward and with one stroke of his axe the king was dead.

This painting, probably largely based on verbal descriptions, records the scene. In the top left corner is the king as he was at his trial. In the vignette beneath, he walks in procession to his execution. In the central

scene the executioner holds up the severed head. A woman in the foreground swoons with horror. In the top right, the executioner, bearing a strong resemblance to the Cromwellian General Fairfax, holds his axe and the severed head, and in the oval below, people dip their kerchiefs in the royal blood, eager to have souvenirs of the occasion.

OPPOSITE
King Charles I as a child *by Robert Peake*
Oil on canvas, 127 × 85.7
Bequeathed by the 13th Baron Elibank in 1973
PG 2212

Susanna Hamilton, Countess of Cassillis 1632–1694
by John Michael Wright

The Hamiltons were for centuries one of the most powerful and important families in Scotland. Susanna's father was the first Duke of Hamilton and King Charles I's principal Scottish adviser. When the king was captured and imprisoned in 1648 the duke led an army south from Scotland to try to rescue him. He failed and was captured, imprisoned and beheaded.

Susanna Hamilton spent her early years at her father's house in Chelsea, then on the edge of London. She was surrounded by the magnificent collection of paintings by Rubens, Van Dyck and Correggio which her father had amassed. During the turmoil of the Civil War she was sent out of London for safety to her grandmother's house.

Susanna Hamilton was thirty and still unmarried when John Michael Wright painted this portrait. She was hardly a beauty, yet this portrait is nevertheless one of Wright's finest.

Five years later, at the age of thirty-five, Susanna married the nineteen-year-old Earl of Cassillis.

Oil on canvas, 72.4 × 61
Dated 1662
Bought in 1986
PG 2687

William Drummond of Hawthornden 1585–1649
attributed to Abraham van Blijenberch

William Drummond's father was a gentleman usher to James VI, and William was brought up among the poets and writers associated with the Court. He was educated at the University of Edinburgh and then continued his studies in London, Bourges and Paris, intending to be a lawyer. However, when his father died, he abandoned his legal career.

He had already started writing poetry, and his first publication, in 1613, was an elegy on Prince Henry Frederick. Other volumes of poetry followed. His mother's brother was the poet William Fowler and he became a friend of Sir William Alexander, likewise known for his poetry. When Ben Jonson, the English playwright, came to Scotland in 1618 he spent a few weeks staying with Drummond at Hawthornden, the property his father had acquired not far from Edinburgh. He himself collected books, and in 1627 made a gift of no fewer than 500 to the library of the University of Edinburgh. Five years later he was busy writing verses for Charles I's visit to Scotland, and began work on a history of the Stewart kings, the *History of Scotland from the Year 1423 until the Year 1542*. His portrait shows him in elegant court dress, with a fine lace collar.

Oil on panel, 60.4 × 48.5
Dated 1612
Bought in 1928
PG 1096

Anne Erskine, Countess of Rothes (died 1640) with her daughters, Lady Margaret and Lady Mary Leslie *by George Jamesone*

The portrait of the Countess of Rothes and her two daughters was painted as a companion to a full-length portrait of John Leslie, 6th Earl of Rothes which Jamesone had painted the previous year. Anne, who was the daughter of the 2nd Earl of Mar (Treasurer Mar) and Marie Stewart, had married Rothes in 1614. Rothes, who carried who carried the sword of state before James VI and I on his visit to the Scottish parliament in 1617, would later support the forces of the Covenant before his early death in 1641, the year after his wife's death.

Besides its interest as a depiction of the clothes and jewellery of a noble Scotswoman and her children, the portrait has a special importance for the information it contains on the appearance of a Scottish interior of its period. It is not likely, however, to be a precise description of a particular room in the original Leslie House. Stylistically, the portrait is evidence of Jamesone's familiarity with the kind of Anglo-Netherlandish portraiture in vogue at the Jacobean court.

Oil on canvas, 219.4 × 135.5
Dated 1626. Bought in 1980
PG 2456

George Jamesone 1589/90–1644 · *Self-portrait*

Oil on canvas, 72 × 87.4
Bought in 1976
PG 2361

George Jamesone is the first major figure in the history of Scottish painting. Although born in Aberdeen, he was trained in Edinburgh by a decorative painter, John Anderson, who was probably a relative. From 1620 Jamesone practised independently as a portrait painter, firstly in the north-east, but he soon gained patronage throughout Scotland. Briefly in the mid-1620s he faced some competition from Adam de Colone, who represented the Netherlandish tradition in Scotland, but thereafter he had a virtual monopoly.

His principal patron in the 1630s, when he worked mainly from premises in Edinburgh, was Sir Colin Campbell of Glenorchy, for whom he painted portraits of members of allied families as well as a series of portraits of ancestors. This kind of semi-decorative portraiture he also provided for the ceremonial entry of Charles I to Edinburgh in 1633.

Jamesone acquired considerable social and artistic status during his lifetime, which finds expression in this self-portrait. His appearance perhaps aping that of his great European contemporary, Rubens, he points to the signs of his wealth and achievement. The painting dates from a year or two before Jamesone's death in 1644 when the political situation, in which he had been involved, was rapidly deteriorating.

Archibald, 8th Earl and 1st Marquis of Argyll 1598–1661 by David Scougall

When Argyll sat for his portrait, the Edinburgh artist David Scougall made no attempt to disguise the squint which earned the sitter the Gaelic nickname 'Gillespie Gruamach' and gave him a somewhat sinister aspect. His restrained, dark garments are perhaps a reflection of the fact that he was leader of the Covenanting party, but his religious convictions did not deter him from pursuing a policy of personal ambition.

He became a privy councillor at the age of twenty-one, but his father was soon warning Charles I that he could become a source of trouble. In 1641 the King, attempting to conciliate the opposition, made him a Commissioner of the Treasury and elevated him from Earl to Marquis, but he continued to support the King's

parliamentary enemies until he himself was three times defeated by the royalist Marquis of Montrose. Shocked at the execution of Charles I, however, Argyll changed sides and it was he who crowned the young Charles II at Scone in 1651. He continued to play a devious game during the Commonwealth period, and when Charles II was restored, he was arrested and executed.

Oil on canvas, 73.7 × 67.3
Bequeathed by the Marquess
of Lothian in 1941
PG 1408

Robert Kerr, 1st Earl of Ancram 1578–1654 by Jan Lievens

The events of Ancram's life seem emblematic of his time, combining cultivated taste and high office with physical violence and great changes in fortune. He succeeded to the family estates at the age of 12 after the assassination of his father. In 1603 he entered the service of King James's eldest son, Henry, Prince of Wales. In 1613 he was appointed Gentleman of the Bedchamber to Prince Charles. He was exiled in 1620 after killing his opponent in a duel but was pardoned six months later. In 1623 he joined Prince Charles in Spain and on Charles's accession he was made Lord of the Bedchamber and subsequently Keeper of the Privy Purse. He was created Earl of Ancram on the occasion of Charles's Scottish coronation in 1633. Ancram remained a faithful royalist and withdrew to Amsterdam after the execution of King Charles. He died there in poverty, his dead body was arrested by his creditors and only released for burial through the mediation of Cromwell.

Ancram was a friend of the poets John Donne and William Drummond and was a poet himself. He was also an imaginative connoissieur of paintings, bringing back from a diplomatic mission to the Low Countries two works by Rembrandt, the first to enter Britain. Lievens, a highly successful portrait painter, was a close friend of Rembrandt, who, according to Ancram, 'hath so high a conceit of himself that he thinks there is none to be compared with him in all Germany, Holland nor the rest of the 17 Provinces.'

Oil on canvas, 62.2 x 51.4 cm
Painted in 1654
On loan from the Marquess of Lothian
PGL 210

General Tam Dalyell c.1599–1685 by L. Schuneman

Oil on canvas,
124.4 × 101.6
Bought in 1967
PG 2129

General Tam Dalyell had a notable military career in the seventeenth century. After service in France and Ireland, he supported Charles I in the Civil War and took part in the 1651 expedition into England led by the young Charles II. Taken prisoner at the battle of Worcester, he was imprisoned in the Tower of London, but he managed to escape and went abroad. He was back in Scotland briefly in 1654 to take part in a rising in the Highlands, but not long after that he entered the Russian army, rising to the rank of general in wars against the Poles and the Turks.

After the Restoration, Charles II recalled him and in 1666 gave him command of the forces in Scotland. He defeated the Covenanters at Rullion Green when they rose against the king, and in 1681 raised the Scots Greys. A colourful figure, it was said that when he heard of the execution of Charles I he made a vow not to cut his beard until the monarchy was restored, and his enemies told tales of him playing cards with the devil at his House of the Binns. This clean-shaven portrait, dating from the 1670s, is attributed to Schuneman, a German artist who visited Scotland.

James Graham, 5th Earl and 1st Marquis of Montrose 1612–1650
attributed to William Dobson

Oil on canvas, 75.6 × 58.4
Bequeathed by Lady Malise
Graham in 1978
PG 2418

Montrose was one of the most romantic figures in seventeenth-century Scotland, a poet as well as a dashing general of Charles I. At first, he had supported the National Covenant, fighting against the king's army in the first and second Bishops' Wars. However, he grew suspicious of his ally Argyll, for he became convinced that the latter was acting out of self-interest rather than a desire for the common good. In 1641 he was imprisoned in Edinburgh Castle on a charge of having conspired against Argyll, and on his release he changed sides. This portrait may have been painted by William Dobson when he was with the king in Oxford from 1643 to 1644.

In the late summer of 1644, Montrose raised the Highland clans for the king, and was joined by the Earl of Antrim with an Irish force. Despite a series of victories in the north, he was routed in 1645 at Philiphaugh, near Selkirk, by an army sent from England. He retired to the Continent, but after the execution of Charles I he came back to Scotland, only to be defeated again, at Carbisdale in April 1650. He was captured during the battle and later hanged in Edinburgh.

Charles II 1630–1685 by William Dobson

Oil on canvas,
153.6 × 129.8
Bought in 1935
PG 1244

In 1643 Charles I and his army fought Parliamentary forces led by the Earl of Essex at Edgehill. The battle was inconclusive, and the king decided to march to Oxford, where he set up his headquarters. Soldiers and noble families occupied the Oxford colleges, and William Dobson set up a studio in a house on the High Street to paint portraits of the fashionable visitors.

One of his most eminent sitters was Charles, Prince of Wales, who had been with his father at Edgehill. Although only twelve years old, he is portrayed in buff jerkin and breast-plate, his sword at his side, a military baton in his right hand, while the battle rages in the distance. His page stands beside him, holding out the prince's helmet. In the lower left corner of the picture is the dreadful head of the Gorgon Medusa, symbol of strife, and the trumpet of the war goddess, Athena.

The prince remained in Oxford until March 1645, when he began to move westwards and eventually sought refuge in Jersey before going into exile on the Continent.

Princess Elizabeth 1635–1650 and Princess Anne 1637–1640
by Sir Anthony van Dyck

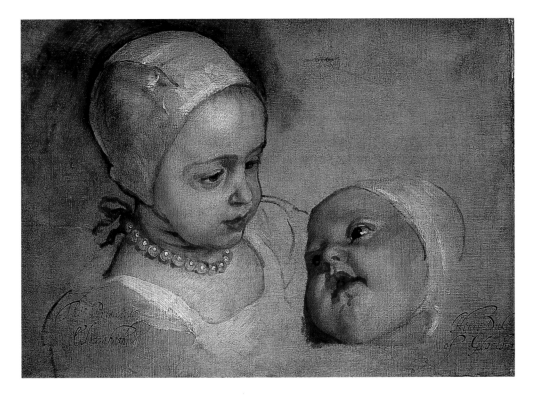

Charles I and Henrietta Maria had four sons and five daughters. This unique oil-study for Van Dyck's famous painting, *The Five Eldest Children of Charles I*, shows two-year-old Elizabeth supporting the baby, Anne. The large group picture, painted for the king in 1637, hung above his breakfast table at Whitehall and is still in the royal collection.

Sadly, neither little girl survived to adult life. Anne died of tuberculosis just after her third birthday. Elizabeth was held prisoner by the Roundheads during the Civil War. A gentle, sensitive child, she never really recovered from the news of her father's execution, and when she was moved to Carisbrooke Castle, the scene of his long imprisonment, she died soon afterwards at the age of fifteen. Like her sister, she had been suffering from tuberculosis, but her mother was convinced that she had died of a broken heart.

The inscription on the picture, which was added at a later date, contains an error. Princess Anne, on the right, has mistakenly been given the name of her brother Henry, Duke of Gloucester.

Oil on canvas, 29.8 × 41.8
Bought with help from the Heritage Lottery Fund, the Scottish Office and the National Art Collections Fund in 1996
PG 3010

Lord Mungo Murray 1668–1700 by John Michael Wright

Lord Mungo, the fifth son of the Marquis of Atholl, a great Highland chieftain, is dressed for hunting. He wears a belted plaid, a double width of tartan cloth about five yards long, unsewn and belted round the body to form a kilt below the waist and a mantle above. He also wears a fashionable doublet, holds a flintlock sporting gun and carries two scroll-butt pistols in his belt. In addition he bears a dirk and a ribbon-basket sword.

Through his mother's family, Lord Mungo was related to the Irish dukes of Ormonde. This portrait appears to have been painted in Ireland in the early 1680s when the young Scotsman was attached to the court of his Irish relatives at Kilkenny Castle, to complete his education. The portrait, which may have been commissioned by the Duke of Ormonde to show a Scotsman in his national dress, has a companion, now in the Tate Gallery in London, showing Sir Neil O'Neil, an Irishman, in his national costume.

Lord Mungo died young, fighting in the vain attempt to establish a Scottish colony in Panama.

Oil on canvas,
224.8 × 154.3
Bought in 1925
PG 997

John Maitland, 2nd Earl and Duke of Lauderdale 1616–1682 by Sir Peter Lely

John
Duke of Lauderdale

Oil on canvas,
124.4 × 101.6
Bought in 1967
PG 2128

Known to his contemporaries as 'Red John', because of his colouring, Lauderdale virtually ruled Scotland on behalf of Charles II. Originally a Covenanter, he had changed sides during the Civil War and after the battle of Worcester was imprisoned in the Tower of London because of his royalist activities. On his release in 1660, he became Secretary of State for Scotland, a position he held for twenty years, exercising considerable influence over the king.

Lauderdale sat for this majestic portrait to Sir Peter Lely, the fashionable court painter, about 1665. Lely also painted a companion portrait of Lauderdale's wife, the rather plain Lady Anna Home, whom the duke was to desert in 1670 after nearly forty years of marriage. He had fallen in love with the beautiful and dangerously ambitious widow, Elizabeth, Countess of Dysart. They married when Lady Anna died, and Lauderdale then built Thirlestane Castle in Berwickshire and Ham House in London, which he and Elizabeth furnished in luxurious style.

During his career the duke made many powerful enemies, and eventually they provoked his downfall. Removed from office, he retired to Tunbridge Wells, where he died in 1682.

John Mylne 1611–1667 by an unknown artist

John Mylne was a member of a famous family of architects, stone masons and engineers. His grandfather had built a bridge over the River Tay at Dundee in the first decade of the seventeenth century, his father worked on the tolbooth in Aberdeen, and his uncle, Alexander, was a sculptor as well as a mason.

John himself was principal master-mason in Scotland by 1636, and it was he who designed the Tron Church in Edinburgh High Street, which opened in 1647. At the same period he was working on part of Heriot's Hospital, now George Heriot's School. Edinburgh College was another of his projects in the mid 1640s, at a time when he was also occupying himself with other, more controversial, concerns. He was an active supporter of the Covenanters, and in 1646 he was made master-gunner in Scotland. He served on Edinburgh Town Council during the Cromwellian period and also after the restoration of Charles II, and he was MP for Edinburgh from 1662 to 1663.

Sir William Bruce c.1630–1710 by John Michael Wright

Sir William Bruce was the leading architect in Scotland during the second half of the seventeenth century. Above all, he is associated with the reconstruction and redecoration of Holyroodhouse in Edinburgh, the chief palace of the Stewart kings in Scotland. At Hopetoun and at Kinross House, which he built for himself, Bruce created the fashion for a new classical style of architecture in complete contrast to the defensive tower houses which were common up to this time.

John Michael Wright trained in Edinburgh with George Jamesone during the late 1630s. In 1642 he went to Rome where he became the only British painter of the century to be elected a member of the Accademia di San Luca, the prestigious academy of artists. Wright was in Rome for at least ten years before leaving for Flanders to become antiquary to the Archduke Leopold, Governor of the Spanish Netherlands.

Both Bruce and Wright, who was a Roman Catholic, prospered during the reigns of Charles II and his brother James VII and II (1660–1688). But when King James was forced into exile by the Protestant King William, the careers of both men suffered.

Oil on canvas, 72.4 × 61
Bought in 1919
PG 894

John Graham of Claverhouse, Viscount Dundee 1648–1689 by David Paton

'Bonnie Dundee' or 'Bloody Clavers', as he was variously known, was an able military commander who, after a time at the University of St Andrews, served in the French and Dutch armies as a volunteer before returning to Scotland in 1678. Those Scots who preferred the presbyterian form of church government to the episcopalian one were causing the government trouble by holding large outdoor meetings known as conventicles, protected by armed guards. Graham was sent with his troop of horse against them, and, although he was defeated at Drumclog, he was part of the force which crushed the conventiclers at the battle of Bothwell Brig. His activities then and in the years which followed earned him a reputation for brutality which was much exaggerated.

When William of Orange invaded England in 1688, Graham supported James VII and II, who created him Viscount Dundee. He urged the king to stay and fight, but James fled to the Continent. Undeterred, Dundee began raising the Highland clans for James and on 27 July 1689 he confronted the government army led by General Hugh MacKay in the Pass of Killiecrankie. His army won a resounding victory, but Dundee was killed and opposition to William faded away.

Pen and ink on paper,
10.5 × 8.3
Gifted by A. Sholto Douglas in 1900
PG 588

Queen Anne 1665–1714 by Willem Wissing and Jan van der Vaardt

Queen Anne was the last of the Stewart dynasty to occupy the British throne. She and her older sister, Mary, were the surviving children of James VII and II by his first wife, Anne Hyde, and were raised on the instructions of Charles II as Protestants. Anne's life was dominated by the religious and political differences between herself, her father and his Roman Catholic son, Prince James Francis Edward Stewart. After James VII was driven out of the country for his religion, the throne was firstly occupied by Mary with her husband, William of Orange, and subsequently by Anne, who was married to Prince George of Denmark, from 1702. Her reign was dominated by war with the French which saw the military victories of her favourite, the Duke of Marlborough, principally at the battles of Blenheim, Oudenarde and Malplaquet. Her notable domestic act was the union of the kingdoms of Scotland and England in 1707.

Oil on canvas,
199.4 × 128.3
Bought in 1922
PG 939

The Solemnization of the Marriage of Prince James Francis Edward Stewart and Princess Maria Clementina Sobieska at Montefiascone on 1 September 1719 *by Agostino Masucci*

Oil on canvas,
243.5 × 342
Bought with help from the
National Art Collections
Fund, the Pilgrim Trust and
private donors in 1977
PG 2415

The dramatic abduction of the Polish princess, Maria Clementina Sobieska, from Innsbruck by a small band headed by Charles Wogan is one of the most romantic episodes in the whole Jacobite story. When the party eventually reached Italy the princess was received with honour and rejoicing. At Bologna, on 9 May 1719, she went through a form of marriage-by-proxy or betrothal with James Murray, Lord Dunbar, representing Prince James Francis Edward Stewart. At that time Prince James was in Spain but he returned to Italy in August that year. He based himself in the small town of Montefiascone in the hills between Bolsena and Viterbo, from where he sent for his bride. They met for the first time on 1 September 1719, and were married between sunset and midnight that evening, the ceremony taking place in one of the saloons of the episcopal palace. The Bishop of Montefiascone, Pompilio Bonaventura, officiated, while the witnesses included John Hay, Lord Dunbar, Charles Wogan and John O'Brien. Princess Clementina was only sixteen, half the age of Prince James, and her bridegroom noted approvingly that she was polite, nicely dressed and, best of all, had not 'so much as a will of her own'. He was mistaken in this last observation, and almost from the start their relationship was a stormy one.

James Carnegie, 5th Earl of Southesk 1692–1730 *by Pier Leone Ghezzi*

During the Jacobite Rising of 1715 Lord Southesk supported Prince James Francis Edward Stewart (the Old Pretender) whom he proclaimed King James VIII at Montrose. He was appointed colonel of a regiment of Angus horse, which he commanded under the Earl of Mar at the battle of Sheriffmuir. Lord Mar described him at the time as 'a very honest man, and zealous servant of our master's.' When the king landed in Scotland, in the winter of 1715/16, he was the guest of Lord Southesk at his seat, Kinnaird Castle, near Brechin. After the failure of the Rising, Lord Southesk was attainted and stripped of all his honours. He escaped to France and made his way to Avignon to join the Jacobite court. He spent the rest of his life either in Italy or Paris. This lively caricature, inscribed on the verso 'Mylord Soudesk', was drawn by Pier Leone Ghezzi in Rome in the last years of the earl's life.

Pen and ink on paper,
31.7 × 22.2
Bought in 1979
PG 2452

Field-Marshal George Wade 1673–1748 attributed to Johan van Diest

Born in Ireland of English settlers, Wade was a professional soldier whose early career enjoyed steady promotion reflecting his distinguished record, mainly on the Iberian peninsula. From the time of the 1715 Rising onwards, however, Wade's military service became inextricably interlinked with Scotland and the Stewart cause. In 1724 he was appointed Commander-in-Chief, North Britain, and was sent to Scotland to reconnoitre the Highlands where he concluded that the main impediment to 'civilising' the region was the want of good communications. During the next eleven years Wade supervised the building of over 250 miles of roads and forty bridges. Labour was provided by a force of 500 soldiers whom Wade called his 'Highwaymen'; he treated them well, providing them with roasted oxen for feasts and equipment for brewing ale.

This painting shows Wade standing before his most spectacular feat of construction, the Corrieyairack Pass (1731) on the road from Fort Augustus to Dalwhinnie and Ruthven. Normally Wade's roads aspired to Roman straightness but, to climb this pass of over 2,500 feet, traverses, supported by stone bulwarks, zigzagged up the mountainside. Poles were inserted at fixed intervals to mark the route when the road was obliterated by snow.

Ironically, the Jacobite armies found these roads immensely convenient in 1745; Bonnie Prince Charlie's army used the Corrieyairack pass on its way south.

Oil on canvas, 75 × 63.2
Bought in 1977
PG 2416

James Gibbs 1682–1754 by Andrea Soldi

Oil on canvas,
111 × 87.5
*Gifted by the National Art
Collections Fund in 1938*
PG 1373

James Gibbs, an Aberdonian, was sent to Rome in 1703 to study for the priesthood at the Scots College. He rapidly abandoned a clerical career and became the pupil of the leading baroque architect in Italy, Carlo Fontana. When he returned to Britain in 1709 his Continental training made him highly sought after and he also enjoyed the patronage of his fellow Catholic and Scot, the Earl of Mar. In 1713 he was appointed Surveyor to the Commissioners for building fifty new churches in London and designed St Mary-le-Strand. This promising official career was cut short by the death of Queen Anne and the establishment of a less sympathetic, Hanoverian and Whig, regime. Gibbs was dismissed from his post but, such was his reputation and experience, that aristocrats, particularly Tories, continued to seek him out, especially for building country houses. While virtually all of these houses are in England, for William Duff, Lord Braco, he built Balveny House (demolished 1929) in Banffshire.

In 1728 Gibbs published *A Book of Architecture*, a volume with 150 engraved plates illustrating his designs. This work was popular and influential, becoming something of a pattern book for Georgian architects and builders in Britain and the American colonies.

Prince Charles Edward Stewart 1720–1788

Prince Charles Edward
Stewart by Maurice-
Quentin de La Tour
Pastel on paper, 61 × 51
Bought with help from the
National Art Collections
Fund in 1994
PG 2954

Prince Charles, the elder son of Prince
James Francis Edward Stewart, was
born and brought up in Rome and
trained for a military life, first seeing
action at the siege of Gaeta in 1734. In
1743, the French government having
offered help, Charles set out from
Dunkirk with a French fleet and 7,000
men in an attempt to regain the throne
of Great Britain for his father, but
storms drove the fleet back and French
help was withdrawn. The prince
decided to rely on support in Britain
and, after raising as much money as
possible, he sailed for Scotland and
landed in the Hebrides in 1745 with
only a few followers. Most of the
Highland clans rose in arms on his
behalf and he was soon able to march
south at the head of a considerable
force. He occupied Edinburgh,
defeated General Cope at Prestonpans,
captured Carlisle, and advanced as far

south as Derby, where lack of support
from the English Jacobites and
discontent in his army persuaded the
leaders that a retreat was necessary. A
withdrawal was started in December
1745. The Jacobite army again
defeated the government forces at
Falkirk, but, greatly weakened by
casualties and desertions, retired
towards Inverness. In April 1746
Prince Charles's army was totally
defeated and dispersed by the
government forces under the Duke of
Cumberland at Culloden. After a
period of hiding in the western
Highlands, Charles escaped to
France and remained in exile for the
rest of his life.

The portrait of the twelve-year-old
prince was painted in Rome in 1732
by Antonio David. The pastel was
drawn in Paris by one of the most
accomplished of all the French
pastellists of the eighteenth century.
It is almost certainly the portrait
referred to as 'Le Prince Edouard',
which La Tour exhibited at the Paris
Salon in 1748, and which, two years
later, the prince bought from the
artist. It is still surrounded by its
original carved and gilded Parisian
frame.

OPPOSITE
Prince Charles Edward Stewart
by Antonio David
Oil on canvas, 73.4 × 60.3
Painted in 1732
Bought in 1918
PG 887

Flora Macdonald 1722–1790 by Richard Wilson

Oil on canvas,
76.4 × 58.7
Bought in 1931
PG 1162

The famous Jacobite heroine Flora Macdonald was the daughter of Ranald Macdonald, a farmer at Milton on the island of South Uist in the Outer Hebrides. In 1746, while on a visit to the Clanranalds, who lived on the neighbouring island of Benbecula, she met Prince Charles Edward Stewart in flight after the disastrous battle of Culloden. She helped the prince to reach the Isle of Skye, but was subsequently imprisoned in the Tower of London after the prince's escape. However, in 1747, she was released under the Act of Indemnity, and in 1750 she married Allan Macdonald. She emigrated to North Carolina in 1774, but returned in 1779 to Scotland.

This portrait, by the Welsh artist, Richard Wilson, who is better known as a landscape painter, was painted in London. After her capture in 1746, Flora Macdonald was a prisoner on board an English man-o'-war for some five months. The captain of the ship, Nigel Gresley, showed her a great deal of kindness. She gave this portrait to him as a mark of appreciation.

Prince Charles Edward Stewart 1720–1788 in disguise as Betty Burke
by J. Williams

Mezzotint engraving on
paper, 32.5 × 22.5
Bought by the Gallery at an
unknown date
SPIV 123–23

After his defeat at the battle of
Culloden in 1746, Prince Charles
Edward Stewart took refuge in the
islands of the Outer Hebrides.
Increasingly, there was danger that he
might be discovered by the large
number of troops dispatched to search
for him. Flora Macdonald was
persuaded to smuggle the prince
across to Skye, disguised as her maid
Betty Burke, 'an excellent spinner of
flax and a faithful servant.'

Despite his renowned pretty looks,
the Prince was, by all accounts,
unconvincing as a woman.

Lord George Murray 1700– 1760 by Sir Robert Strange

Lord George, a younger son of the 1st Duke of Atholl, was already an experienced military commander when he joined Bonnie Prince Charlie in 1745. He led the Jacobites to victory at Prestonpans but he and the prince clashed constantly. Charles was proud and imperious, while even Lord George's friends had to admit that he was 'fierce, haughty and blunt'. Their relationship reached its lowest point when he advised the prince to retreat from Derby. After Culloden, where he fought bravely, Lord George escaped to the Continent and spent the rest of his life in exile. This sensitive miniature was drawn by Sir Robert Strange, himself an ardent Jacobite, who was present throughout the campaign.

Pencil and ink on paper,
9 × 7.3
Bought in 1988
PG 2754

Simon Fraser, Lord Lovat c.1667–1747 by William Hogarth

William Hogarth went to see Lord Lovat, the eighty-year-old chief of Clan Fraser, while he was in custody in St Albans, en route to be tried for high treason in London.

Lovat had led an unprincipled life, forcibly marrying his first wife after having failed to abduct her nine-year-old daughter, an heiress. In politics, he adroitly and surreptitiously switched his support to and fro between the Jacobites and the British government. Eventually, in 1746, he was wrong footed, having brought out his clan to fight for Prince Charles at Culloden. Lovat's support for the Jacobites was incontestable and he was captured in hiding soon after the battle.

A contemporary who witnessed Hogarth and Lord Lovat together described the artist's portrait: 'The old Lord is represented in the very attitude he was in while telling Hogarth and the company some of his adventures.' The artist latter stated that he depicted Lovat counting the numbers of the clans who supported the prince on his fingers, while he detailed the numbers of men each clan chief had mustered.

Lord Lovat was tried, found guilty and beheaded on Tower Hill. Hogarth is believed to have printed some 10,000 copies of this portrait which were sold for a shilling a print.

Etching on paper, 36.7 × 23.7
Published in 1747
Acquired by the Gallery at an unknown date
SPIII 53/10

Allan Ramsay 1686–1758 by William Aikman

The poet Allan Ramsay was born at Leadhills in Lanarkshire, the son of the lead-mining manager on Lord Hopetoun's property. At the age of fifteen he was apprenticed to a wig-maker in Edinburgh. Starting business on his own, he soon became a citizen of substantial means and a noted figure in the Jacobite 'Easy Club', founded in 1712. Six years later he abandoned wig-making in favour of book-selling and from then on wrote and published the poetical works on which his reputation now rests. His collection, The Tea-Table Miscellany, appeared in 1724, but most famous of all was The Gentle Shepherd, a pastoral poem first published the following year. After 1730 he laid aside his pen, fearing, as he said, 'the cooling of fancy that attends advancing years'. He married Christian Ross, the daughter of an Edinburgh lawyer, and his family consisted of three sons and five daughters, of whom Allan, the elder son, the portrait painter, is the best known.

This portrait was in the collection of Sir John Clerk of Penicuik, an eminent lawyer and antiquarian, who was a patron to both Ramsay and Aikman. Sir John was the author of the following lines, which were inscribed on the back of the canvas:

> Here painted on this canvass clout
> By Aikman's hand is Ramsay's snout
> The picture's value none might doubt
> For ten to one I'll venture
> The greatest criticks could not tell
> Which of the two does most excell
> Or in his way should bear the bell
> The Poet or the Painter.'

Oil on canvas, 75.7 × 64
Dated 1722
Bought in 1924
PG 973

Allan Ramsay 1713–1784 · *Self-portrait*

*Pastel and watercolour on
paper, 40.6 × 28.2
Gifted by the Royal Scottish
Academy in 1910*
PG 727

The son of the poet of the same name, Allan Ramsay was born in Edinburgh and received his first artistic training at the city's Academy of St Luke. His father, ambitious for his talented son, raised the funds to send him to Rome. There he studied at the French Academy and drew alongside the up and coming artist, Pompeo Batoni. In Naples, Ramsay was taken into the studio of the illustrious painter, Francesco Solimena.

On his return, Ramsay based himself in London but kept a studio in Edinburgh to which he returned most years during his father's lifetime. Through the influence of the Earl of Bute, Ramsay was introduced to the Prince of Wales and on the latter's accession to the throne as King George III, became the king's painter. As well as a consummate portrait painter, Ramsay was highly regarded by his contemporaries as an essayist and conversationalist. An accident to his right arm in 1773 cut short his painting career.

Anne Bayne, Mrs Allan Ramsay d.1743 by Allan Ramsay

Oil on canvas, 68.3 × 54.7
Bought in 1983
PG 2603

Allan Ramsay's portrait of Anne Bayne was probably painted in Edinburgh in the late 1730s, at the time the couple were engaged to be married. Their marriage was postponed until after the artist had returned from a two-year visit to Italy, where his style was radically transformed. This portrait of his demure fiancée, the daughter of a professor at the University of Edinburgh, and the granddaughter of the architect Sir William Bruce, is the masterpiece of Ramsay's early style. But while Anne Bayne is beautifully observed and exquisitely painted, the portrait is still provincial in its stiffness. Anne died in 1743 giving birth to her third child. The artist remarried nine years later and had a second family.

Anne Ruddiman d.1769 by William Denune

Oil on canvas, 76.2 × 63.7
Gifted by Miss S. Stewart
in 1962
PG 2012

Anne Smith was born the daughter of Thomas Smith who traded as a woollen draper in London and then married the heiress to a brewery in Edinburgh. She married the classicist, librarian and printer, Thomas Ruddiman, in 1729, and probably brought him considerable wealth. The marriage contract secured for her an annuity of 10,000 merks (roughly £500 sterling, a considerable sum for the day). She was Ruddiman's third wife and the portrait was painted in 1749 as a companion to a picture of her husband. She bore him two children but only one survived to adult life.

After her husband's death she is known to have defended her interest in his highly successful publication, *Rudiments of the Latin Tongue*, and she printed the seventeenth edition of this work, with a print run of 20,000 copies, shortly before her own death in October 1769. She was described as 'a woman of fine aspect, elegant manners, and amiable disposition.'

Sir James Macdonald 1741–1766 and Sir Alexander Macdonald c.1745–1795 *attributed to William Mosman*

Oil on canvas,
176.5 × 147.3
Bought in 1967
PG 2127

The two boys, James on the right and Alexander on the left, were the sons of Sir Alexander Macdonald of Macdonald, a great Highland chieftain with estates on the Isle of Skye. Although the portrait is likely to have been painted in Edinburgh, it is probably Skye that the artist intended to evoke in the background.

The boys are shown at sport: James with his gun, Alexander playing golf. By the mid eighteenth century golf in its modern form was already a well-established pastime in Scotland.

Of great interest is the children's costume. Sir James wears the modern little kilt, whilst his brother wears trews. Between them, they sport three different patterns of tartan. Individual family or clan patterns did not become widely established until towards the end of the eighteenth century.

William Inglis c.1712–1792 by David Allan

Oil on canvas,
129.5 × 105.1
Bought in 1961
PG 1971

William Inglis was a surgeon and three times President of the Royal College of Surgeons. In his spare time, he was a golfer and the Captain of the Honourable Company of Edinburgh Golfers.

The artist, David Allan, himself a member of the same golf club, has painted Inglis wearing the uniform of the Honourable Company, accompanied by his young caddy who holds his clubs. They are shown on Leith Links, about two miles from the centre of Edinburgh. The Links had been a favourite place for golf since at least the sixteenth century. In 1744 the City of Edinburgh presented an annual prize to be played for by members of the Honourable Company. The trophy, a golf club with silver balls attached, was paraded through the city before the competition. Allan has shown the procession with the town officer holding the trophy accompanied by two drummers. The portrait was painted in 1787.

Sir Hew Dalrymple, Lord Drummore 1690–1755 by Allan Ramsay

Oil on canvas,
127 × 102.5
Dated 1754
Bought with help from the
National Heritage
Memorial Fund and the
National Art Collections
Fund in 1989
PG 2800

For much of his life Allan Ramsay had studios in both London and Edinburgh and, while spending most of his time in England, usually came north to Scotland each year for a month or two. At the end of 1753, however, Ramsay turned his back on London to spend almost a year in Edinburgh, where he took a prominent position in the brilliant intellectual life of the city. In 1754 he and the judge, Lord Drummore, were founder members of the prestigious Select Society, a forum for intellectual debate. The painter and the judge were also closely involved with the Edinburgh Musical Society and this portrait was commissioned in the same year by the Society for its concert hall, St Cecilia's Hall. Soon after he had completed this portrait Ramsay left for three years in Italy. Lord Drummore died the following year. At his funeral concert the Dead March from *Saul* and excerpts from other oratorios by Handel were sung.

William Hamilton of Bangour 1704–1754 *by Gavin Hamilton*

William Hamilton of Bangour is shown in profile within a painted circular frame surrounded by laurel leaves. He wears classical dress. The imagery, based on antique coins and medals, is used to indicate Hamilton's status as a poet, celebrated for his translation of Homer. The fictive bas-relief below the portrait illustrates an episode from Hamilton's poem, 'Contemplation or the Triumph of Love'. The seated figure is the poet himself. The allegorical message of the scene, as in the portrait above, is that William Hamilton's poetic work will long survive the death of the poet.

Gavin Hamilton, who painted this picture, was William Hamilton's cousin. At the start of his career the poet had helped the young painter to travel to Italy and had suggested Roman artists under whom he might study. Gavin Hamilton remained in Italy for most of his life, a pioneer of neo-classical painting and a leading archaeologist. This portrait was probably painted in France in 1748 on one of Gavin Hamilton's rare journeys back to Scotland. His cousin was there in exile after supporting the Jacobite Rising three years earlier.

Oil on canvas, 91.6 × 71.2
Bequeathed by W.F.
Watson in 1886
PG 310

Sir William Chambers 1723–1796 by Francis Cotes

Pastel on paper,
63.5 × 48.2
Dated 1764
Bought in 1904
PG 629

William Chambers was born in Stockholm, the son of a Scottish merchant. At the age of sixteen he visited China where his interest in architecture was kindled. His career paralleled that of his fellow architect and great rival, Robert Adam. After travelling on the Continent in the 1750s he found advancement from the patronage of Lord Bute and the position, with Adam, as one of the two joint architects in the Office of Works in London. Between 1752 and 1762 Chambers made his reputation with his designs, for Princess Augusta, of the grounds and buildings at Kew. His pagoda there helped establish the vogue for 'chinoiserie' in furniture and ornament design. Never as fashionable as Adam, he was instead the greatest official architect of his day. He exerted great influence in his profession and was the first treasurer of the Royal Academy of Arts.

His most ambitious project, rivalling Adam's nearby Adelphi, was the building of Somerset House on the Thames. In Edinburgh he built Duddingston House and Dundas House in St Andrew Square, now the headquarters of the Royal Bank of Scotland.

Robert Adam 1728–1792 by James Tassie

Robert Adam was the son of William Adam, the most successful Scottish architect of the early eighteenth century. While he inherited his father's considerable abilities as an entrepreneur and businessman, Robert surpassed him as an architect.

Adam spent three years, in his mid twenties, in Italy and the contacts he made there, both among artists and future patrons, formed the basis of his later success. Important too was his five-week reconnaissance of the remains of the palace of the Emperor Diocletian at the Adriatic port of Split.

Adam's initial employment on his return to Britain came mainly from patrons who wanted to remodel their country houses. The originality of Adam's solutions and his inventive use of classical motifs appealed greatly to his clients.

Much of Adam's Scottish work belongs to the second half of his career. Register House (1772–92) and Old College in Edinburgh (begun in 1789) helped transform and dignify the capital. Adam's castle buildings, of which Culzean is perhaps the finest example, demonstrate his ability to make use of quite disparate architectural sources and integrate them in a picturesque composition.

Paste medallion, 7.8 high
Dated 1792
Bought in 1887
PG 262

David Hume 1711–1776

David Hume
by Louis Carrogis, called Carmontelle
Pencil, red chalk and watercolour on paper,
30 × 17.3
Bought in 1974
PG 2238

The great philosopher and historian was painted twice by Ramsay, firstly, in 1754, when Hume was the Keeper of the Advocates' Library in Edinburgh, and secondly, in this portrait of 1766 when Hume had returned to Britain from three years in France.

It was painted as a companion to a portrait Hume had commissioned earlier that year from Ramsay of the French philosopher Jean-Jacques Rousseau. Hume had assisted Rousseau's flight from France, found him accommodation in England and secured him a pension from the king. Despite these favours Rousseau quarrelled bitterly with Hume.

In this portrait, where the light directed on Hume's head may symbolise knowledge, and the darkness behind him, ignorance, Ramsay has shown Hume's right hand resting on two books. One of these is a volume of the Roman historian, Tacitus, an allusion to Hume's *The History of England* published between 1754 and 1757. The other is untitled. It may be intended to remind the viewer of Hume's philosophical publications, such as his *Treatise on Human Nature* (1739–40), works in which he established an empirical system of philosophy which had enormous influence.

The witty sketch of Hume by Carmontelle was drawn in Paris a little earlier than Ramsay's portrait. Hume held the position of secretary to the British ambassador to the French court between 1763 and 1766.

OPPOSITE
David Hume by Allan Ramsay
Oil on canvas, 76.2 × 63.5
Bequeathed by Mrs Macdonald Hume of
Ninewells to the National Gallery of Scotland in
1858 and transferred
PG 1057

Professor Francis Hutcheson 1694–1746 by Antonio Selvi after Isaac Gosset

Bronze medal, 10.5 diameter
Cast in 1746
Bought in 1910
PG 699

In the eighteenth century a durable medallic portrait was thought to be a particularly appropriate way of recording for posterity the features of poets and philosophers, those men – and in the eighteenth century it was almost exclusively men – whose writings were expected to endure. As Alexander Pope wrote:

> *The medal, faithful to its charge of fame,*
> *Thro' climes and ages bears each form*
> *and name.*

This medal of the great philosopher Francis Hutcheson was commissioned in Florence by one of his pupils, Basil Hamilton, later Earl of Selkirk. On the reverse of the medal, the genius of philosophy is shown mourning the death of Hutcheson.

Francis Hutcheson was born and educated in Ulster, the grandson of an Ayrshire man who had settled there. But Hutcheson is most closely associated with Glasgow, and with the University of Glasgow in particular. He was a student there for six years and returned in 1729 to the chair of moral philosophy, remaining professor until his death.

Hutcheson had great influence, particularly on the Scottish philosophers of the 'common sense' school. His formula, 'the greatest happiness for the greatest number,' was adopted by Jeremy Bentham and the utilitarians later in the century.

William Hunter 1718–1783 by Edward Burch

It was the advice of the great physician, William Cullen, that steered William Hunter to a career in surgery. After studying divinity at the University of Glasgow, Hunter became Cullen's resident pupil in Hamilton. After a few months with Alexander Monro ('Munro Primus') in Edinburgh, Hunter moved to London where he remained for the rest of his life.

His own teaching attracted the attention of students and society alike: Edward Gibbon, Edmund Burke and Adam Smith were among many non-specialists who attended his lectures. In 1762 Hunter was consulted by Queen Charlotte and two years later he was appointed her Physician Extraordinary, consolidating his position as the leading obstetrician in Britain. In 1768, he became the first Professor of Anatomy to the Royal Academy of Arts. Hunter's most important published work was entitled *On the Human Gravid Uterus*, handsomely illustrated with engraved plates, the production of which had been supervised by Sir Robert Strange. Strange also helped Hunter form a magnificent collection of coins, works of art, scientific specimens and ethnographic items which was bequeathed to his old university in Glasgow.

Copper medal, 8 diameter
Bought in 1985
PG 2647

John Campbell, 4th Duke of Argyll 1693–1770 by Thomas Gainsborough

'Handsome Jack Campbell', as he was known in his youth, did not inherit his cousin's dukedom until he was sixty-seven. Before that, he was a professional soldier and in 1745 it was his task to defend the west of Scotland against Prince Charles Edward Stewart's forces. After the battle of Culloden, he led the sea search for the prince to the Outer Hebrides, sailing as far as St Kilda. Although Prince Charles Edward eluded him, Campbell did arrest many of those who had helped the prince, including Flora Macdonald. In 1746, Campbell succeeded the Duke of Cumberland as commander in Scotland, and 'pacified' the Highlands.

In this magnificent portrait by Thomas Gainsborough, the artist has shown Argyll wearing his peers' robes and the Order of the Thistle, and also carrying the baton of Hereditary Master of the King's Household. Rarely was Gainsborough so sensitive to the poise of intrepid old age and to nuances of a face that looks to an uncertain future.

Oil on canvas, 235 × 154.3
Bought in 1953
PG 1596

James Boswell 1740–1795 *by George Willison*

James Boswell's father was a staid and steady judge and for much of his life there was conflict between the lawyer's sensible plans for his son and the latter's extravagant schemes and licentious behaviour. In the summer of 1763, under threat of disinheritance, James Boswell left Scotland to study law in Holland. The law, however, was soon abandoned and for Boswell Holland was a mere springboard into the very tempting pool of eighteenth-century Europe. He visited Berlin and Paris, met Jean-Jacques Rousseau and Voltaire and became a fervent friend and supporter of Paoli, the Corsican nationalist. In Rome, Boswell commissioned a history painting from Gavin Hamilton and, in 1765, sat for his portrait to George Willison, a Scottish pupil of Anton Raphael Mengs.

On his return to Britain, Boswell renewed his early acquaintance with Dr Samuel Johnson and so began a lifelong friendship, immortalised in Boswell's *Life of Samuel Johnson*, often acclaimed as the greatest biography in the English language.

*Oil on canvas,
135.2 × 96.5
Bequeathed by Captain
James Wood in 1912*
PG 804

James Bruce of Kinnaird 1730–1794 by Pompeo Batoni

*Oil on canvas, 72.4 × 62.2
Bequeathed by Lady
Ruthven in 1885*
PG 141

With a height of six feet four inches James Bruce, explorer, archaeologist and linguist, was a commanding figure. His 'grand air, gigantic height and forbidding brow awed everybody into silence ... He is the tallest man you ever saw gratis', wrote the novelist, Fanny Burney.

Pompeo Batoni, the portraitist of so many languid and callow young men passing through Rome on their Grand Tour, appears to have relished the challenge to paint someone with character. Bruce's portrait was painted in the summer of 1762 when he was spending six months in Italy, travel-ling south to take up the post of British Consul in Algiers. Bruce was already a seasoned traveller and had mastered Arabic and Ethiopic. Algiers provided the base for archaeological expeditions along the North African littoral. From there he travelled to Crete and Syria and in 1768 he arrived in Egypt to sail up the Nile to Aswan. He crossed the desert to the Red Sea, visited Abyssinia and explored the sources of the Blue Nile.

James Byres 1734–1817 and members of his family by *Franciszek Smuglevicz*

To the ever changing tourist population of eighteenth-century Rome James Byres was one of the modern landmarks of the city. The son of committed Jacobites and a Roman Catholic, Byres left his family estate at Tonley in Aberdeenshire after the 1745 Jacobite Rising to be brought up on the Continent. In 1758 he moved to Rome where he trained as a painter under Mengs and studied architecture. His practical knowledge of these two arts was useful to him when he established himself as one of the leading art dealers and professional guides in the city.

One of Byres's best known clients was Edward Gibbon who was introduced to the antique ruins of imperial Rome in an arduous course of visits and lectures lasting many weeks. Byres's greatest coup as a dealer was probably the purchase for the Duke of Rutland of Poussin's *Sacraments* from the Boccapaduli collection. This portrait shows Byres, second from the left, with members of his family. His sister Isabella, Mrs Robert Sandilands, stands beside him. Her husband died in 1775 and she is shown wearing mourning. On the far right of the canvas is Charles Norton, a relation of Byres and a business associate. Byres's parents, Patrick and Janet, are shown third and fourth from the left.

Oil on canvas, 63.2 × 75.8
Bought with help from the National Art Collections Fund in 1983
PG 2601

Lord Fortrose 1744–1781 at home in Naples by *Pietro Fabris*

'We went to Lord Fortrose, with whom we were to dine', wrote Charles Burney in November 1770, 'but first I was to see his medals, cameos, intaglios, Etruscan vases, pictures etc which I did with great delight. It is impossible for anyone to do the honours of his house better than Lord Fortrose – we were all at our ease, all cheerful and happy.' Lord Fortrose, later Earl of Seaforth, is the central figure in both small paintings, which show two different views of the same room in his Neapolitan apartment.

The paintings are a unique visual record of the cultured and comfortable life of the British in Italy in the eighteenth century. Fortrose and his friend William Hamilton, the British envoy in Naples, provided a welcome to any Briton passing through the city. Patrick Brydone, who appears behind the lunging fencer, described the hospitality thus: 'After bathing [off Fortrose's boat] we have an English breakfast at his Lordship's and after breakfast a delightful little concert, which lasts for an hour and a half. Barbella, the sweetest fiddle in Italy, leads our little band. This party, I think, constitutes one principal part of the pleasure we enjoy at Naples.'

The artist, who has depicted himself painting the concert, has also recorded two musicians who were visiting Naples for six weeks in the summer of 1770. Leopold Mozart is playing Fortrose's own British-built harpsichord while his son Wolfgang Amadeus Mozart, reading off his father's music, plays a little octave spinet, supported on a chair.

OPPOSITE
Oil on canvas, each 35.5 × 47.6 cm
Dated 1771
*Bought with help from the National Art
Collections Fund in 1984*
PG 2610 & PG 2611

Lady Charlotte Campbell 1775–1861 by Johann Wilhelm Tischbein

Lady Charlotte was the daughter of Elizabeth Gunning, Duchess of Hamilton and Argyll, who was a noted beauty. Her father, the 5th Duke of Argyll, was himself the son of another beautiful woman, Mary Bellenden. Lady Charlotte inherited her family's good looks and the artist Tischbein was captivated: 'Sometimes I had the opportunity to paint people who were more perfect than the best artist could have imagined them and who rivalled the most beautiful ideals – I had this good fortune with Charlotte Campbell.'

Tischbein's memorable encounter with his sitter occurred outside Naples at the close of a royal hunt. Lady Charlotte was there to watch the spectacle, but as the carriages were starting to leave the forest the fifteen-year-old girl got caught up in the traffic and panicked, running desperately from the path of one vehicle to the next. Seeing her, Tischbein was reminded of the friezes of dancers at Herculaneum and saw in her frenzied beauty an image from the classical past come to life.

Lady Charlotte married Colonel John Campbell in 1796. Subsequently, she married the Revd Edward John Bury, under whose surname she achieved considerable success as a novelist.

Oil on canvas, 197.2 × 134
Bought in 1975
PG 2275

Jane Maxwell, Duchess of Gordon c.1749–1812 by *George Romney*

Jane Maxwell, the daughter of a Wigtownshire baronet, was born in Edinburgh where she is said to have been a boisterous child, riding on the backs of pigs that ran loose in the wynds of the Old Town. She grew up to be beautiful, witty and ambitious. Married to the 4th Duke of Gordon, she helped run the vast family estates, bore seven children and became a leader of fashionable society in London and Edinburgh. She was a confidante of Pitt and her Pall Mall home was the social hub of the Tory party. Her political socialising was successful to the extent that she married three of her five daughters to dukes, and a fourth to a marquess. Latterly, she became bitterly estranged from her husband. Described in his youth as 'one of the handsomest men of his day', the Duke of Gordon had a large second family by a mistress, Jane Christie, whom he married after Jane Maxwell's death.

In Romney's outstanding portrait of 1778, the duchess is shown with her elder son, George, Marquess of Huntly (1770–1836). Before he succeeded to the dukedom in 1827, he pursued a successful and distinguished career in the army. His mother is said to have helped him recruit tenants on the family estates by offering the king's shilling from between her lips.

Oil on canvas,
126.4 × 102.5
Painted in 1778
Bought with help from the
Pilgrim Trust in 1972
PG 2208

Alexander Runciman 1736–1785 and John Brown 1749–1787
by Alexander Runciman

Oil on canvas, 63.6 × 76.5
Dated 1784
On loan from the Society of
Antiquaries of Scotland
PGL 31

This curious double portrait of two
highly original, romantic artists was
painted as a gift for their eccentric
patron David, Earl of Buchan who
formed a collection of portraits of
notable Scots which he called his
Temple of Caledonian Fame.

Both Runciman, seated on the left,
and Brown, holding a copy of
Shakespeare's The Tempest, had been
in Rome around 1770 where they
found kindred spirits in artists such
as Fuseli, Sergel, Abildgaard and
Barry. On their return to Scotland,
Runciman was employed to paint a
large mural cycle for Penicuik House
showing scenes from the mythic tales
of Ossian. Brown specialised in both
life-size and miniature portrait

drawings, all of great quality.

Brown wrote about this painting to
Lord Buchan in August 1784: 'I was
yesterday with Runciman and sat for
my portrait which he has done a first
sitting on the same canvas on which he
has already done his own. The piece is
for your Lordship and I think will be an
admirable one. He has represented
himself sitting at his work, his pallet
and pencils in one hand and a porte
crayon in the other. I, behind, am
seeming to point at and find fault with
some part of his work, at which as
being rather irascible and impatient of
reproof, he is making a damnable face,
as he expresses it. I flatter myself your
Lordship will be much satisfied with it.'

Robert Fergusson 1750–1774 by Alexander Runciman

Fergusson's first poems, in English, were published by Water Ruddiman in *The Weekly Magazine* in 1771. They were followed by 'The Daft Days' and 'Auld Reekie' in a vigorous Scots which attracted much attention. During his lifetime Fergusson's reputation was confined to his circle in Edinburgh. Later, however, his importance was recognised by Robert Burns who saw him as his essential precursor and who erected a monument to him in the Canongate Kirkyard.

This portrait has an old inscription on the back identifying it as Fergusson: 'Supposed to be the only one extant and to be done by Runciman the intimate friend of the Poet'. This may well be correct but the possibility remains that it is a study for, or a fragment of, a subject picture – Runciman is rumoured to have painted Fergusson for inclusion in a painting of 'The Prodigal Son'.

Oil on paper mounted on millboard, 26.7 × 21.3
Bought in 1959
PG 1863

Robert Burns 1759–1796

Robert Burns
by Alexander Reid
Watercolour on ivory,
7.6 × 6.3
Bequeathed by W.F.
Watson in 1886
PG 341

Robert Burns was born at Alloway in Ayrshire, the son of a farmer who provided him with an excellent education. On the death of his father in 1784, Burns tried his hand at farming, but met with little success. While Burns considered emigration, he wrote a number of his finest poems: 'The Twa Dogs', 'The Cotter's Saturday Night', and 'To a Mouse' all date from 1785. He hoped that by publishing his work, in the now famous Kilmarnock edition of his poems (1786), he would raise the money to establish himself in Jamaica. But such was the success of the edition that he decided to remain in Scotland and he was lionised by Edinburgh society. It was while Burns was in Edinburgh that Alexander Nasmyth painted this portrait, now the most

famous image of the poet. Introduced to each other by their mutual acquaintance and patron, Patrick Miller of Dalswinton, Burns and Nasmyth became good friends. The portrait was commissioned by the publisher William Creech, to be engraved for a new edition of Burns's poems. Apparently Nasmyth never quite completed the portrait, preferring to leave it unfinished rather than take the risk of losing his likeness.

Alexander Reid's miniature portrait belongs to the last eighteen months of the poet's life. By this time Burns was living in Dumfries, working as an exciseman, another farming venture at Ellisland on the Nith having proved a failure. Early in 1795, Burns described Reid's portrait to a friend: 'I am just sitting to Reid in this town for a miniature; and I think he has hit by far the best likeness of me ever was taken.'

The poetry of Robert Burns, both in Scots and English, has become an important part of Scottish national identity. His personality – democratic and generous – has also become an ideal for many Scots.

OPPOSITE
Robert Burns
by Alexander Nasmyth
Oil on canvas, 38.4 × 32.4
Bequeathed by Colonel William Burns in 1872
PG 1063

Henry Dundas, 1st Viscount Melville 1742–1811 by David Martin

Oil on canvas,
127.6 × 101.6
Painted in 1770
Bought with help from the
National Heritage
Memorial Fund and the
National Art Collections
Fund in 1988
PG 2745

Following family tradition, Henry Dundas trained as an advocate. His career at the Scottish bar was brief and he moved speedily into politics. Solicitor-General at the age of twenty-four, Lord Advocate at thirty-three, he became the 'intimate friend and trusted lieutenant' of the Prime Minister, William Pitt, over a considerable period of time. Dundas was active principally in naval, Indian and Scottish affairs. The Dictionary of National Biography states that 'for nearly thirty years he was the most powerful man in Scotland, and, as the election agent for the government, controlled the elections of the Scotch representative peers, as well as the Scotch members for the House of Commons'. No one north of the border in the eighteenth century was as powerful as the man who was widely known as 'Harry the Ninth, the uncrowned King of Scotland.'

Professor Adam Ferguson 1723–1816 by Sir Joshua Reynolds

As Professor of Natural Philosophy and then Moral Philosophy at the University of Edinburgh, Ferguson was a central figure of the Scottish Enlightenment. He was a friend of David Hume and married the niece of the eminent professor of chemistry, Joseph Black. Ferguson was eloquent and popular as a professor, his lectures attracting an audience from well beyond the confines of the university. His writings include contributions to political and ethical thought, and the great nineteenth-century historian, Thomas Carlyle, considered that he was 'particularly well worth reading on Roman history'. He has been credited as being a pioneer of the discipline of sociology and an influence upon Hegel and Marx.

Ferguson's career was, however, hardly narrowly scholastic, and in this he is typical of his intellectual milieu. As a young chaplain to the Black Watch he had published a sermon (preached to the regiment in Gaelic) denouncing the Pretender, Catholicism and France. He travelled extensively in Europe, met Voltaire at Ferney, and in 1778 went on an (unsuccessful) diplomatic mission to negotiate with the American colonists at Philadelphia. Ferguson also worked as a farmer, implementing agricultural improvements, and it was at his Edinburgh home, in the winter of 1786/7, that the young Walter Scott met Robert Burns for the first and only time.

Oil on canvas, 75.9 × 63.5
Bought in 1992
PG 2890

James Watt 1736–1819 by John Henning

Chalk on paper, 53 × 43.8
Dated 1809
Gifted by Miss M. Campbell
in 1891
PG 294

The 'watt', the term used to describe a unit of power equal to a rate of one joule per second, takes its name from this prolific inventor and engineer. James Watt is an archetypal figure of Britain's industrial revolution, a man of no great formal education who studied theoretical science, via experimentation, for practical ends which were then put to commercial use.

Born in Greenock, Watt trained as a maker of mathematical instruments and worked in this capacity for the University of Glasgow from 1757. Within this environment he became familiar with the work of Professor Joseph Black, the discoverer of latent heat. In 1764 a Newcomen engine was sent to him for repair; faced with this, Watt applied the theories of Black and was able to improve the apparatus, primarily through the means of a separate condenser. Watt made several other improvements which entitle him to be considered as the father of the steam engine as an effective instrument of practical application.

Watt pursued his inventions within several business alliances, most importantly in partnership with Matthew Boulton at the Soho Works, Birmingham. When living in Birmingham, in the milieu of Joseph Priestley and Josiah Wedgwood, Watt made the discovery that water was not an element but a compound of oxygen and hydrogen.

Joseph Black 1728–1799 by David Martin

Oil on canvas, 126.8 × 102
Dated 1787
On loan from the Royal
Medical Society, Edinburgh
PGL 259

Joseph Black was born in Bordeaux, the son of a Scots wine merchant. He was a student in Glasgow, where he became an assistant to the physician, William Cullen. Later he would succeed Cullen both at Glasgow and Edinburgh universities, in the former as Professor of Medicine, in the latter as Professor of Medicine and Chemistry. Black's thesis, published in 1754 as 'Experiments upon Magnesia Alba, Quicklime and some other Alkaline Substances', was a document of great importance in laying the foundation of quantitative analysis and of pneumatic chemistry. Black developed the fundamentally important theory of 'specific heat', which paved the way for James Watt's improvements to the steam engine. Joseph Black was a great teacher and in later life a prominent member of intellectual society in Edinburgh, numbering among his friends Adam Ferguson, David Hume and Adam Smith. He acted as a physician to many of his friends and was also widely employed as an industrial consultant.

This portrait of Joseph Black was commissioned by the Royal Medical Society of Edinburgh.

Adam Smith 1723–1790 by James Tassie

The name of Adam Smith is today synonymous with the economic principle of free enterprise. His most influential work, *The Wealth of Nations*, published in 1776, described how the individual pursuit of self-interest leads to the common good. In this book, Smith also proposed labour, and not land, as the source of national wealth and theorised the 'division of labour' as a basis of production. Smith was, however, a more complex intellectual figure than his posthumous popular reputation suggests. He was greatly influenced by Francis Hutcheson, whom he followed as Professor of Moral Philosophy at the University of Glasgow and he shared the ethical concerns of his great friend, David Hume.

A native of Kirkcaldy, Smith was briefly kidnapped by gypsies as a child, but otherwise his private life was unremarkable and typical of the many convivial characters of the Scottish Enlightenment. While travelling in France as the tutor to the young Duke of Buccleuch, he met Voltaire and was a great hit with the ladies of the Paris salons; in London he socialised with Samuel Johnson's circle and in Edinburgh he founded a dining club with the two scientists, Joseph Black and James Hutton.

Paste medallion, 7.5 high
Dated 1787
Bought in 1886
PG 157

Robert Foulis 1707–1776 by James Tassie

Robert Foulis was publisher to the University of Glasgow. In 1754 he and his brother Andrew founded a school of fine arts housed in the College of Glasgow. Known as the Foulis Academy, its teaching was based on Continental models, and it was one of the earliest art schools in Scotland. Robert Foulis formed a collection of Old Master paintings, casts and prints, which the students were encouraged to copy. Among the principal components of the curriculum were the study of anatomy, geometry and perspective; the intended goal was the creation of history paintings, then considered the highest level of fine art. The students did not have to pay fees, but were treated like apprentices, with some scholars supported on study tours of Italy, subsidised by wealthy benefactors in Glasgow. When this patronage declined in the early 1770s, the Foulis Academy suffered financially, and it was eventually closed in 1775. The picture collection was later sold at auction in London. The two most prominent students of the Academy were the genre painter and portraitist David Allan, and the creator of the portrait in glass paste, James Tassie.

Paste medallion, 4.1 high
Bought in 1886
PG 137

James Tassie 1735–1799 by David Allan

David Allan and James Tassie were fellow students at the Foulis Academy in Glasgow in the early 1760s. While Allan's career developed along conventional lines, becoming a painter and illustrator, Tassie invented a new medium for miniature reproductive portraiture which he also employed for making casts of antique gems and cameos. Allan's portrait shows Tassie holding his own reproduction of the Strozzi Medusa.

Tassie's products were sought by collectors all over the world. Catherine the Great was his most important patron. Manufacturers like the potter Josiah Wedgwood and the Swedish silversmith Andrew Fogelberg also used his work to enhance their products.

For a short while in the late 1770s Tassie and Allan shared a house in London. They jointly marketed their products, advertising together in the Press. David Allan moved back to Scotland, to become the head of the Trustees' Academy in Edinburgh. To Allan and his pupils, James Tassie's career must have seemed exemplary and inspiring. A boy of modest background, trained like themselves in Scotland, by an intelligent application of science to art, he perfected his medium to rise above his competitors and become a leader in his field.

Oil on canvas, 76.6 × 64.9 Bequeathed by William Tassie to the National Gallery of Scotland and transferred in 1898
PG 576

David Allan 1744–1796 by Domenico Corvi

Oil on canvas, 74.3 × 61.3
Dated 1774
Gifted by the Royal Scottish
Academy in 1910
PG 731

Throughout his life David Allan was supported by a network of influential and inter-related families of which the most important were the Cathcarts and Erskines of his native Alloa. It was through their help that he studied art at the Foulis Academy in Glasgow and with their support that he was able to spend ten years in Italy. Artistically these were the most successful of his life and in 1773 he won the Concorso Ballestra at the Academy of St Luke in Rome with the *Departure of Hector*. Classical subject matter, however, was less his forte than genre scenes. He recorded the street life of Rome and Naples with a witty eye and pretty touch. His set of drawings of the Roman carnival were engraved in aquatint by Paul Sandby.

Domenico Corvi, the Roman artist under whom Allan may have studied, has shown the Scot painting from a cast of the Borghese Gladiator.

James Hutton 1726–1797 by Sir Henry Raeburn

Oil on canvas,
125.1 × 104.8
Bought with help from the
National Art Collections
Fund and the National
Heritage Memorial Fund in
1986
PG 2686

Hutton is considered the founder of modern geology. The son of an Edinburgh merchant, he was educated at the High School and the universities of Edinburgh, Paris and Leiden, from where he gained the degree of M.D. in 1749. He subsequently farmed near Duns in Berwickshire, returning to Edinburgh about 1765, where he lived at St John's Hill in the Pleasance. His business included property, a partnership in a successful sal-ammoniac plant (using soot collected by chimney sweeps) and membership of the Forth and Clyde canal committee. His enquiring mind embraced chemistry, philosophy, phonetics, meteorology and agriculture, but he was chiefly attracted to geology, a pursuit he developed while farming.

In his now-famous paper, *Theory of the Earth*, delivered to the Royal Society of Edinburgh in 1785, he showed that continents are gradually being worn away to form new continents on the sea floor; that the interior of the Earth is hot; and that the processes that shape the Earth operate extremely slowly over a very long period of time. Indeed, Hutton could see 'no vestige of a beginning – no prospect of an end' to the geological history of the Earth.

Sir James Hall 1761–1832 by Angelica Kauffmann

A pioneer of geology, Sir James Hall's contribution to this science resulted from his practical observations, experiments in the laboratory and fruitful encounters at home and abroad with colleagues and friends such as Lavoisier and James Hutton. From 1783 to 1785 he made a Continental tour, investigating rock formations in the Alps and Apennines and studying the volcanoes, Etna, Vesuvius and Stromboli. Hall sat to Kauffmann in Rome towards the end of his stay in Italy.

Hall was typical of the age in the breadth of his interests. He published a book on the origins of Gothic architecture in which he argued that both the essentials and details of the style derived from masons reproducing primitive wattle structures in stone. A pointed arch resulted from the binding of two flexible branches, and elements such as crockets and cusps from copying the sprouting buds and curling bark of the fresh wood. To test his theory he constructed (with the help of a local cooper) a miniature 'cathedral' of willow branches in the grounds of Dunglass, his estate on the East Lothian-Berwickshire border. The effect was both picturesque and convincing, the only problem being that, by the following year, the 'Willow Cathedral' was alive, many of the rods having taken root.

Oil on canvas, 60.5 × 49.5
Bought with help from the National Art Collections Fund in 1994
PG 2990

Niel Gow 1727–1807 by Sir Henry Raeburn

Oil on canvas,
123.2 × 97.8
Bought in 1886
PG 160

Gow, the son of a plaid weaver from Inver in Perthshire, was a largely self-taught fiddler of great virtuosity. His compositions and arrangements were enormously popular and he published several collections, including a *Collection of Strathspey Reels* in 1784. As a fiddler, he was especially acclaimed for the strength of his 'up-bow', or returning stroke, 'which never failed to surprise and delight'. He was also noted for 'the sudden shout' which often accompanied his playing and which was said to electrify dancers.

A major influence on the development of Scottish folk music, he was taken up by the aristocracy and the Duke of Atholl and the Duchess of Gordon were particular patrons. The poet, Robert Burns, visited Gow and his wife in 1787 and described him as 'a short, stout-built, honest highland figure, with his grayish hair shed on his honest social brow – an interesting face, marking strong sense, kind open heartedness mixed with unmistrusting simplicity'.

Matthew Hardie 1755–1826 by Sir William Allan

Matthew Hardie was an important and influential violin maker, who has been called the 'Scottish Stradivari'. Born in Edinburgh, he probably trained as a cabinet or pattern maker. His instruments, which always followed the Stradivari model, were praised for both their beauty and quality of tone. From his premises on Calton Hill, Hardie also dealt in old violins and undertook repairs. Although renowned as the foremost maker in Scotland, towards the end of his life Hardie's business was undercut by cheaper factory imports and he spent some time in a debtor's jail. He died in St Cuthbert's Poor-house. His skills, however, had been passed on to his son, Matthew, and his cousin, Paul, in what was to become a dynasty of violin makers.

Hardie preferred to find wood that had already been aged for his violins. One contemporary anecdote tells how Hardie, in a farmhouse kitchen, spotted an old baking-board made of maple. 'I see, mistress, ye have a fine fiddle here', commented Hardie. The woman assured him that there was no such thing in her house, but, if he could find one, he could have it. Hardie's reply was to take the baking-board and make from it the 'hidden fiddle'!

Oil on panel, 26.7 × 22.9
Bought in 1960
PG 1955

Robert Macqueen, Lord Braxfield 1722–1799 by Sir Henry Raeburn

Oil on canvas,
120.6 × 100.3
Bought in 1954
PG 1615

Robert Macqueen was said to be the best feudal lawyer in Scotland, expert in intricate legal questions arising out of the forfeitures subsequent to the 1745 Rising. His posthumous fame, however, owes more to his reputation as a 'hanging judge', the model for Lord Hermiston in Robert Louis Stevenson's unfinished novel, *Weir of Hermiston*. As Lord Braxfield, he presided over the trial of Muir, Skirving and Margarot for sedition in 1793. The bias of the proceedings and the harshness of the sentences led to criticisms being made in Parliament. Reactionary in politics and a hard drinker, Braxfield was acknowledged by friend and foe alike as a 'giant' of the bench, notorious for uttering such memorable aphorisms as, 'Hang a thief when he's young, and he'll no steal when he's auld'.

These quips were delivered in lively Scots, leading Stevenson to comment (as he looked at this portrait), 'He was the last judge on the Scottish bench to employ the pure Scotch idiom. His opinions, thus given in Doric, and conceived in a lively, rugged, conversational style, were full of point and authority ... He left behind him an unrivalled reputation for rough and cruel speech; and to this day his name smacks of the gallows'.

Thomas Muir 1765–1799 *by David Martin*

Born in Glasgow, the son of a prosperous merchant, Muir attended his native university where he was taught by John Millar, Professor of Civil Law, an intellectual leader of the Scottish republican Whigs. After expulsion from the University of Glasgow, Muir finished his studies at Edinburgh and was called to the bar in 1787. As a young advocate he acquired a reputation for defending the oppressed. Encouraged by the revolution in France, Muir was at the forefront of agitation for parliamentary reform, and formed a society for this purpose in 1792. Muir was a fine orator who made clear the relation between support for radicalism and freedom for Scotland. Already marked by the authorities as a dangerous man, Muir was arrested on charges of sedition in 1793. While on bail he went to Paris to plead for the life of the French king. Muir was too late and, in the interim, the date of his trial was deliberately brought forward to make him an outlaw.

Muir returned of his own volition a few months later and stood trial in Edinburgh before Lord Braxfield. Accused of 'exciting a spirit of disloyalty and disaffection', and of recommending Thomas Paine's *Rights of Man*, Muir was sentenced to fourteen years' transportation and sent to Botany Bay. In 1796 Muir arranged his escape to America, sailing across the Pacific. Detained by the Spanish, he was then taken to Cadiz where his ship was attacked by the British fleet. Although the ship was captured, Muir, who was terribly injured, was assumed to be dead and he was able to make his way to France. When he reached Paris in 1798 Muir was welcomed by the great painter, Jacques-Louis David, and hailed as a hero and martyr. In the remaining months of his life he tried to persuade the French to help establish a Scottish republic.

Chalk on paper, 29.8 × 18.6
Bequeathed by W.F. Watson in 1886
PG 1668

Adam Duncan, 1st Viscount Duncan of Camperdown 1731–1804
by Henri-Pierre Danloux

Duncan came from a family of pro-Hanoverian Scots. His father, a local landowner, was Provost of Dundee before and after the Rising of 1745 and the next generation all pursued careers in the service of the crown. Adam, the youngest son, joined the Royal Navy in 1746. He served under Admiral Keppel off Africa and the West Indies in his twenties and thirties, and, recalled to active service in 1778, saw action with Admirals Rodney and Howe. During peacetime he lived as an Edinburgh gentleman and made a useful marriage to Henrietta Dundas whose uncle became Pitt's secretary of state for war in 1794.

Until 1796 Duncan's career was worthy rather than remarkable, but during his last posting, he emerged, spectacularly, as one of Britain's great naval heroes. To counter the threat of aggression from the newly created Dutch Republic during the war against France, a North Sea fleet had been formed with Duncan at its command. After successfully blockading the Dutch fleet and despite the serious mutinies of 1796 and 1797, he led his ships to victory off the Dutch coast on 11 October 1797. This victory was significant both practically – the threat of a French invasion now faded – and symbolically, as a huge morale boost after years of inconclusive engagements and domestic discontent.

Oil on canvas, 269 × 195.8
Dated 1798
Bequeathed by the Earl of Camperdown in 1919 to the National Gallery of Scotland and transferred
PG 1065

Sir Ralph Abercromby 1734–1801: The Battle of Alexandria
by Philip James de Loutherbourg

After Nelson defeated Napoleon's fleet at Aboukir Bay in August 1798, the French army in Egypt was left virtually stranded. A British expedition, commanded by Sir Ralph Abercromby, landed in Egypt on 8 March 1801. The ensuing battle of Alexandria, fought on 21 March, put an end to Napoleon's Egyptian empire and with it the threat to British India and Britain's other territories east of Suez. De Loutherbourg, a Swiss landscape painter, who was also a leading stage designer in London, painted the moment during the battle when Sir Ralph was mortally wounded. He died a national hero.

Abercromby, from Clackmannan-shire, originally studied law. In 1756 he switched to the army, working his way up through the ranks from cornet to commander-in-chief in Scotland by 1798.

Oil on canvas,
106.6 × 152.6
Dated 1802
Bought in 1986
PG 2680

Lieutenant-General Sir John Moore 1761–1809 by James Northcote

Oil on canvas, 95.7 × 71.1
Bought in 1936
PG 1301

Moore saw service as a soldier in America, Europe and Africa. His career is a typical, if exceptionally dynamic, example of the energy expended by Britain during the many military campaigns of the later years of the eighteenth century and the early years of the nineteenth. The son of a Glasgow physician, he showed an early inclination to military life. As a boy, during travels in Europe, he once explained to his father how to take Geneva. He joined up at fifteen and became captain-lieutenant to the Hamilton regiment in 1778, the first of a series of promotions that led to his becoming lieutenant-general in 1805.

Moore participated at many of the scenes of conflict during the French revolutionary wars, including Corsica, St Lucia, Holland, Egypt and Sicily. He was so frequently wounded in action that he earned himself the sobriquet of 'unlucky man'. In 1808 he led his troops from Portugal into Spain. Advancing towards Madrid, he learnt that Napoleon had already entered the city and that the French, with superior numbers, had cut off their line of retreat. Moore marched his men through mountainous winter condi-tions back to La Coruña where they were attacked by General Soult before they could embark. The French were defeated but Moore was fatally injured. Napoleon was generous in his praise of Moore and was of the opinion that his efforts alone saved the British army from destruction in Spain.

Major-General James Stuart c.1735–1793 by George Romney

James Stuart was painted by Romney towards the end of a career of mixed fortunes. He first saw active service at the siege of Louisbourg in Nova Scotia in 1758, later fighting in the West Indies, at Martinique and Cuba. In 1715 Stuart joined the East India Company. Second in command on the Coromandel coast, he was suspended by the directors of the company after arresting the governor of the Madras presidency, Lord Pigot. Stuart was later acquitted at a court martial and restored to chief command in Madras. In July 1781 he lost a leg at the battle of Pollilore.

Owing to his alleged mismanagement of the expedition against the town of Cuddalore, Stuart was suspended by Lord Macartney, the governor of Madras. Back in Britain Stuart fought a duel with Macartney in June 1786 and, despite his disability, managed to wound Macartney severely.

This portrait was begun three months later. Stuart sat thirteen times. Comparisons with portraits of the general by other artists suggests that Romney flattered him.

Oil on canvas,
151.1 × 118.7
Bought with help from the
National Art Collections
Fund in 1956
PG 1832

John Rennie 1761–1821 by Sir Henry Raeburn

Oil on canvas, 76.2 × 63.5
Bought with help from the
National Art Collections
Fund in 1957
PG 1840

John Rennie was an East Lothian man and the founder of a family that achieved a great reputation in civil engineering during the nineteenth century. He was born at Phantassie in 1761 and educated at Dunbar and at the University of Edinburgh; later he took up an engagement with the engineering firm of James Watt. Rennie's most important successes were in the field of harbour, dock and canal construction. In terms of sheer size, his greatest work was the mile-long breakwater at Plymouth containing almost four million tons of stone; but he is also remembered for the London Docks, Hull Docks, Lancaster Canal and the dockyards at Chatham among many major constructions. Apart from work of this sort, John Rennie was a bridge-builder of note. Waterloo Bridge, London Bridge and Southwark Bridge in the south, and Kelso Bridge and Musselburgh Bridge in Scotland all bear witness to his skill. The bridge at Musselburgh in fact represented a considerable step forward in design on account of the flatness of the roadway carried over such a long span.

John Loudoun McAdam 1756–1836 by Augustin Edouart

The inventor of the road-building system to which he gave his name, McAdam was the son of a minor Ayrshire laird. He spent his youth in New York, returning to Scotland in 1783, having made enough money to buy an estate and live as a country gentleman. His interest in roads may have been triggered by his serving as a trustee of the Ayrshire turnpike and was confirmed by his uncomfortable experiences travelling between the south-west of England and Scotland on business. Roads, he said, should be smooth, hard and flat in surface (existing rubble-built roads were anything but), and this could be achieved by a composition of small broken stones, arranged in thin layers. As traffic passed over, the surface would become impacted, making it solid and durable.

McAdam had the chance to put his theory into practice when, at the age of sixty, he became surveyor-general of Bristol roads. As well as employing a more satisfactory means of construction, McAdam also introduced efficiencies in the management of the building process. He wrote several books on road-making and was appointed general-surveyor of roads in 1827, the year this silhouette was cut. McAdam's son James succeeded his father as the nation's expert on road-building but their considerable achievements were overshadowed by the growing dominance of the railway.

Silhouette, 26.9 high
Bought in 1913
PG 823

Sir Walter Scott 1771–1832

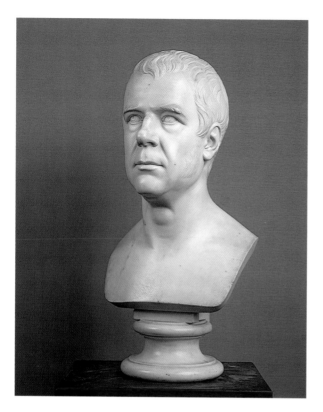

Sir Walter Scott 1771–1832
by Bertel Thorvaldsen
Marble bust, 58 high
Bought with help from the National Heritage
Memorial Fund and the National Art
Collections Fund in 1993
PG 2933

OPPOSITE
Sir Walter Scott 1771–1832
by Sir Henry Raeburn
Oil on canvas, 76.2 × 63.5
Bought with help from the National
Art Collections Fund in 1935
PG 1286

As a result of an illness in childhood (which left him with a permanent limp), Scott was sent from his Edinburgh home to convalesce at his grandfather's farm near Kelso. Here began the passionate love of Border tales and ballads which inspired Scott's brilliant literary career. Scott had trained as a lawyer but the success of poems such as *The Lay of the Last Minstrel* (1805), *Marmion* (1808), and *The Lady of the Lake* (1810) enabled him to buy a country estate. Scott then turned to writing prose, exploring the period of Scottish history during the Stewart and Jacobite years, in novels such as *Waverley* (1814) and *The Bride of Lammermuir* (1819). The contemporary popularity of these works is demonstrated by Jane Austen's wry comment that 'Walter Scott has no business to write novels, especially good ones. – It is not fair. – He has Fame and Profit enough as a Poet, and should not be taking the bread out of other people's mouths'. Later critics saw Scott as the inventor of the historical novel and particularly acclaimed his use of the Scots language in the dialogue of Lowland characters. Subsequent novels turned to other periods and locations. Raeburn's celebrated porrait was painted in 1822 at the zenith of Scott's career. After 1826, he was bankrupted through his association with his publishers, and his work suffered from the need to produce bestsellers in quick succession.

As Scott's health deteriorated, partly as a result of this effort, he set off for Italy in 1831 hoping that the climate would be beneficial. In Rome in 1832, he met the Danish neo-classical sculptor, Thorvaldsen, and the result of this meeting of two of the greatest figures of the age was this marble bust which was completed by 1834.

Sir Walter Scott 1771–1832: The Abbotsford Family by Sir David Wilkie

Oil on panel, 28 × 37.6
Dated 1817
Transferred from the
National Gallery of
Scotland in 1936
PG 1303

'I have been making a little group while here of Mr Scott, Mrs Scott, and all the family, with Captain Ferguson, and some other characters', wrote Wilkie from Abbotsford in August 1817. 'The misses Scott are dressed as country girls, with pails as if they had come from milking: Mr Scott as if telling a story, and in one corner I have put a great dog of the Highland breed, a present to Mr Scott from the Laird of Glengary. In the back-ground the top of the Cowdenknowes, the Tweed and Melrose (as seen from a hill close by) are to be introduced ... I have never been in any place where there is so much real good-humour and merriment. There is nothing but amusement from morning till night; and if Mr Scott is really writing "Rob Roy", it must be while we are sleeping.'

Walter Scott's authorship of the Waverley novels was still unrevealed at this time. Wilkie continued to his sister: 'The family here are equally in the dark about whether Mr Scott is the author of the novels... They hope he is the author, and would be greatly mortified if it were to turn out that he was not... He has denied the Novels, however, to various people that I know; and though the family used to tease him at first about them, yet they dare not do it now.'

Sir Adam Ferguson 1771–1855 by William Nicholson

Oil on canvas
76.2 × 63.5
Bought in 1884
PG 4

Adam Ferguson was the friend and companion of Sir Walter Scott who described him as combining 'the lightest and most airy temper with the best and kindliest disposition.' While Scott studied for the bar – later becoming the most famous writer in Europe – Ferguson joined the army and served under the Duke of Wellington in Spain. Scott liked to recall, with great pride, that his friend had read the description of the battle from Scott's *The Lady of the Lake* to his troops as they were under French bombardment at Torres Vedras.

William Nicholson, who moved from Northumberland to become a central figure in the newly-established Scottish Academy, painted Ferguson's portrait in 1817. Ferguson was, at the time, living as a tenant of Scott and through his influence had been given the honorific title of Keeper of the Regalia of Scotland.

Thomas Campbell 1777–1844 by Sir Thomas Lawrence

Pencil and watercolour on paper,
24.4 × 17.6
Bought in 1926
PG 1034

Thomas Campbell was born and educated in Glasgow. He was the youngest of eleven children, born after his father's tobacco trade had been ruined by the American War of Independence. He considered both the church and the law as careers, but with the success of his poem *The Pleasures of Hope*, published in 1799, he turned to writing full-time. The following year he toured Europe, finding among contemporary events (including the battle Hohenlinden) and new acquaintances, material for his work. Returning to Britain, he settled in London and started on a critical anthology, *Specimens of the British Poets*, briefly with Walter Scott as co-editor.

Campbell was highly thought of in his day and his name was spoken of alongside those of Wordsworth, Byron and Southey. His verse was often used for recitation and quoted, especially his first poem with the famous line, 'tis distance lends enchantment to the view', but it was felt that he never achieved his full potential. Scott, who praised the ballad *Hohenlinden* as being 'devilish fine', made this judgement of his friend: 'the brightness of his early success is a detriment to all his further efforts. He is afraid of the shadow that his own fame casts before him.'

George Gordon, 6th Lord Byron 1788–1824 by William Edward West

Byron's mother, Catherine Gordon of Gight, was a Scottish heiress, but 'Mad Jack', his father, squandered her fortune and the early part of Byron's childhood was spent in modest circumstances in Aberdeen. He was later to say, 'I was born half a Scot and bred a whole one', and a trace of a Scottish accent remained throughout his life. After inheriting his uncle's title he went to Harrow and Cambridge and published his first collection of poems in 1807. This was criticised by *The Edinburgh Review*, causing Walter Scott to remonstrate, saying that the work contained 'passages of noble promise'. This was fulfilled by *Childe Harold* (1812) which made him a darling of society. However, his separation from his wife and hints of an incestuous relationship with his half-sister made him too much the rebellious hero for polite society and, in 1816, Byron left Britain forever.

In Italy Byron continued to write, usually living surprisingly abstemiously (he hated his tendency to plumpness), until, in 1823, he joined the Greek nationalists in their struggle against the Turks. His death, a year later from fever, confirmed his status as a symbol of romantic struggle. West found Byron to be a poor sitter and Countess Guiccioli, Byron's lover, considered this picture to be 'a frightful caricature'.

Oil on canvas, 72.4 × 62.2
Gifted by Colonel William Stirling of Keir in 1951
PG 1561

Professor John Wilson 1785–1854 by Thomas Duncan

Both in mind and body, John Wilson was a larger-than-life character. An essayist and sportsman, one of the founders of the right-wing *Blackwood's Magazine*, he was, for over thirty years, Professor of Moral Philosophy at the University of Edinburgh.

Duncan's portrait shows the sportsman, gun in hand, on the moors. On the page he could be just as deadly, his reviews wounding reputations and killing promising careers. To his contemporaries he must have appeared as a survival from the more boisterous world of the early eighteenth century. To his friends he was 'a true upright, knocking-down, poetical, prosaic, moral, professional, hard-drinking, fierce-eating, good-looking, honourable and straightforward Tory'. He frequently wrote under the pseudonym 'Christopher North'.

Oil on millboard,
60.6 × 42.5
Gifted by the National Art
Collections Fund in 1938
PG 1369

James Hogg 1770–1835 by Sir John Watson Gordon

James Hogg had little formal education, which makes the range and
quality of his literary output all the
more surprising. Born on a farm at
Ettrick, he had ambitions to be a writer
from an early age and came to believe
that he might emulate Burns. He was
still working as a shepherd when his
first, unsuccessful, volume of poems
appeared in 1801. The following year
he met Scott who would champion
him over many years.

Hogg's appearance on the literary
scene was established by *The Queen's
Wake*, which came out in 1813. Many
times reprinted, it contains his most
quoted piece of verse, 'Kilmeny'.
Thereafter his work ranged from the
brilliant parodies of contemporary
poets in *The Poetic Mirror* to the works
in prose: *The Brownie of Bodsbeck*, *The
Three Perils of Man* and, most remarkable of all, *The Memoirs and Confessions of
a Justified Sinner*, which introduced the
theme of the evil doppelgänger into
Scottish literature.

He contributed to *Blackwood's
Magazine* over many years and was
himself portrayed there as 'the Ettrick
Shepherd' in John Wilson's hilarious
sketches, 'Noctes Ambrosianae'.
Watson Gordon's portrait, which
hints at both poet and shepherd, was
painted in 1830 to hang in
Blackwood's salon.

Hogg's last work of note was
*Domestic Manners and Private Life of Sir
Walter Scott* which was published two
years after Scott's death – to the
annoyance of Scott's biographer,
Lockhart – and shortly before Hogg's
own death. He was buried in Ettrick
churchyard.

Oil on canvas, 127 × 101.6
Bought in 1987
PG 2718

William Burke 1792–1829 and William Hare 1790–1860
by T. Clerk after Lutenor

WILLIAM BURKE.

as he appeared at the Bar.

taken in Court.

WILLIAM HARE.

as he appeared in the witness box.

taken in Court.

Engravings on paper,
each 14.5 × 10
Acquired by the Gallery at
an unknown date
SPV 33–2

Burke and Hare are the most notorious criminals in Scottish history. In the early nineteenth century there was a lucrative trade in robbing the graves of the newly deceased to sell the bodies for medical research. In 1827, when one of the lodgers in Hare's house died leaving some rent unpaid, Burke and Hare sold the body to the anatomist, Dr Robert Knox. From this chance beginning, Burke and Hare graduated to murder. They would get their victims drunk, smother them to make it seem they had died from natural causes, then take their bodies to Dr Knox's house.

Their career ended on Hallowe'en 1828, when the frantic cries of their final victim were overheard. The subsequent trial attracted enormous public interest. Only Burke was convicted and hanged. Hare turned 'King's evidence' and walked away free.

Dr Robert Knox 1791–1862 by Augustin Edouart

Robert Knox was a prominent
anatomist and ethnologist in Edinburgh who is best remembered for his
connection with the notorious body
snatchers, Burke and Hare. They
murdered their prey, selling their
bodies to Knox for dissection. There
were political undertones in the
treatment of the men concerned: the
lower-class Irish immigrants Burke
and Hare were tried, whereas the
influential Dr Knox was not charged
with any offence, even though Burke
and Hare's final victim was found on
his dissecting table. Burke loyally
refused to incriminate Knox, saying
only that when he purchased one of
the bodies, 'Dr Knox approved of it
being so fresh, but did not ask any
questions.' Asking no questions may
have been enough for the law, but
public opinion was less forgiving –
there were public demonstrations
outside Knox's house, and his effigy
was later burnt at Portobello.

Silhouette,
18.6 high
Bought in 1913
PG 831

Patrick Grant 1713–1824 by Colvin Smith

Oil on canvas, 126 × 101
Bought in 1993
PG 2924

When King George IV came to Edinburgh in 1822 he was the first British monarch to visit Scotland since Charles I in 1633. This was also the first visit by any member of the royal house of Hanover since 1746, when George IV's great-uncle, the Duke of Cumberland, had decisively defeated the Jacobite army at the battle of Culloden. Memories of the defeat, and of Cumberland's savagery after the battle, were still vivid, eighty years later.

As a young man, Patrick Grant had fought on the Jacobite side against the Hanoverian army. He was 109 when he was introduced to the king as 'His Majesty's oldest enemy'. The king offered Grant and his daughter a state pension, one of many acts of his aimed at reconciling England and Scotland and strengthening the new nation of Great Britain. This portrait was commissioned by William Maule, on whose estates in Angus, Grant and his daughter lived. Painted in 1822, it is one of the earliest and most successful portraits by Colvin Smith, himself a native of Angus.

Carolina Oliphant, Baroness Nairne 1766–1845 and her son William
by Sir John Watson Gordon

Lady Nairne wrote some of Scotland's most famous songs, based on traditional airs. She was born into one of the country's most staunchly Jacobite families and given the christian name Carolina, the feminine form of Charles, as a mark of devotion to Prince Charles Edward Stewart, 'the young pretender', who had been forced into exile twenty years earlier.

Much of her work was inspired by the example of Robert Burns's adaptations of older Scottish songs. She shunned the limelight, publishing her songs in *The Scottish Minstrel* under the name 'Mrs Bogan of Bogan'. These were re-published after her death as *Lays of Strathearn* and included many that are still well-known: the lament for Prince Charles, 'Will ye no' come back again', 'Charlie is my darling', 'The Land o' the Leal', 'The Hundred Pipers', 'Caller Herrin'' and 'The Laird o' Cockpen'.

William succeeded his father as Lord Nairne in 1829. His health had always been delicate and in Watson Gordon's portrait he seems to clasp his mother for support. He spent time with her in France, Italy and Switzerland in an attempt to improve his health, but he died in Brussels in 1837 at the age of twenty-nine.

Oil on canvas, 90.9 × 70.2
Bequeathed by K. Oliphant in 1903
PG 610

Elizabeth Hamilton 1757–1816 by Sir Henry Raeburn

Oil on canvas, 88.8 × 69.8
Bought with help from the
National Art Collections
Fund in 1947
PG 1486

Raeburn appears to have painted Elizabeth Hamilton in mid sentence, not posing for her portrait but engaged in conversation. Absent-mindedly, she plays with a snuff box, her right arm resting on a writing desk on which a pen and ink well can be seen.

Mrs Hamilton, as she was known, although she never married, was brought up by relations in Stirlingshire. She used her knowledge of life in rural central Scotland when she wrote her most famous novel, *The Cottagers of Glenburnie*, which was published in 1808, a few years before this portrait was painted.

In another of her works, *Hindoo Rajah*, Mrs Hamilton examined British society through the critical eyes of a foreigner. In this she was assisted by the letters she received from her brother Charles, who served in India for many years.

Anne Grant of Laggan 1755–1838 by Augustin Edouart

Anne MacVicar was born in Glasgow but spent her childhood in New England before returning to Scotland in 1768. In 1779 she married the Reverend James Grant, minister of the parish of Laggan, in Inverness-shire. Intrigued by Highland culture, she learned Gaelic, studied the domestic habits and folklore of her husband's parishioners and wrote frequent letters about her observations to her friends. When her husband died in 1801, leaving her with eight children, she supported her family by writing, first publishing a volume of poetry. Four years later *Letters from the Mountains* appeared, a selection of her correspondence describing her life in Laggan. Benefiting from fashionable society's fascination with the Highlands, the work was a great success. By the time she moved to Edinburgh in 1810 her reputation was established and she became a dominant figure of the city's literary set. Writing to a friend in 1814, she correctly surmised that Walter Scott was the author of *Waverley*, going on to say that she felt he painted an unjustly violent picture of Highland manners. Scott, for his part, described her as 'so very cerulean' (by which he meant a bluestocking) and 'a woman whose tongue and pen are rather overpowering'.

Silhouette, 16.5 high
Bought in 1932
PG 1177

Andrew Geddes 1783–1844 · *Self-portrait*

Oil on canvas, 76.2 × 62.9
Bequeathed by the artist's
widow to the National
Gallery of Scotland and
transferred in 1898
PG 577

Unlike his contemporary and rival Sir David Wilkie, Andrew Geddes began his career as a painter comparatively late in life. His father was a deputy auditor of excise and, after a classical education at the University of Edinburgh, Andrew Geddes followed in his father's footsteps.

At the age of twenty-three, however, he had become a student at the Royal Academy in London. By 1810 Geddes was already well enough established as an artist to open his own studio in Edinburgh, close to those of both Henry Raeburn and Alexander Nasmyth, in York Place.

This self-portrait is not dated but is believed to have been painted in about 1815. The year previously, both Geddes and Wilkie had been in Paris, admiring the masterpieces that Napoleon had brought together from all over Europe. Geddes was a knowledgeable enthusiast of the Old Masters and this portrait, with its rich colours and vigorous brush work, reflects the influence of some of the great Flemish and Venetian painters whose work he admired in the Louvre.

Sir David Wilkie 1785–1841 · *Self-portrait*

Oil on canvas, 76.5 × 63.5
Gifted by J. Rankin in 1898
PG 573

His gaze directed at the viewer, the young artist grips a portfolio with one hand and holds his porte-crayon in the other. David Wilkie was only twenty when he painted this portrait, but he had already made his mark in Scotland with his vivid portraits of the men and women of his native Fife, and by recording, in part humorous, part documentary manner, the activities of his country neighbours.

This self-portrait was probably the last work Wilkie painted before settling in London in 1805. There, he quickly established himself as the master in paint of psychological drama. Pictures such as *The Blind Fiddler* or *The Letter of Introduction* rely on facial and bodily expression as well as incidental detail to tell their story. In this, Wilkie was the forerunner of much of the anecdotal art of Victorian Britain.

In his later career Wilkie turned his back on his earlier, meticulous style and moved from the influence of David Teniers and other Northern, realist painters to become closer to the great Italian and Spanish masters of the sixteenth and seventeenth centuries with their resonant colours and broader effects.

William Yellowlees 1796–1855 · *Self-portrait*

Oil on panel, 24.1 × 19.7
Dated 1814
Bequeathed by G. Yellowlees
in 1934
PG 1247

William Yellowlees, who specialised in small-scale portraits, was born at Mellerstain in Berwickshire and trained under another Borders artist, William Shiels. For about fifteen years, Yellowlees practised in Edinburgh and took part in the formation of the Scottish Academy. He was known as 'the Little Raeburn', an acknowledgement of the quality of his portraits as much as a comment on their size. This portrait dates from Yellowlees's Edinburgh years.

In the late 1820s he moved to London where he enjoyed considerable success. He was appointed cabinet portrait painter to the enlightened Duke of Sussex, brother of King George IV. Yellowlees was also a regular exhibitor at the Royal Academy in London.

Sir Robert Liston 1742–1836 by Sir David Wilkie

Oil on panel, 30.5 × 25.4
Dated 1811
Bought in 1937
PG 1313

Wilkie painted Liston's portrait in London in 1811 when the diplomat had returned to Britain from The Hague, in preparation for his final posting to Constantinople.

Sir Robert began his distinguished career as the tutor to the sons of Sir Gilbert Elliot. When one of them entered the diplomatic service, Liston became his private secretary and thus began his own career in the service. He held senior appointments in Madrid, Stockholm and Washington, spoke ten languages fluently and, at his death, was known as 'the father of the diplomatic body throughout Europe.'

Mary Somerville 1780–1872 by Pierre-Jean David d'Angers

The daughter of a lowland naval officer, Mary Fairfax received the education then thought fitting for young ladies – very little, with an emphasis on needlework and dancing. Through a combination of quiet determination and natural brilliance, she taught herself, becoming one of the period's foremost mathematicians. She achieved most renown through her expository accounts of current scientific researches, her book, *The Mechanism of the Heavens*, published in 1831, being used as a text book in universities throughout the nineteenth century, while *On the Connexion of the Physical Sciences* (1834) ran to ten editions. Less familiar outside the intellectual circles in which she moved was her experimental work in the field of physical chemistry. Her explorations of the possible magnetizing properties of solar rays, although not confirmed by later scientific work, were considered particularly original and interesting.

During a visit to Paris in 1833 Mary Somerville was introduced to the fashionable portrait and monumental figure sculptor, David d'Angers, by the secretary of the French Academy. The resulting bronze portrait medallion, which achieved great popularity in the scientific community, was considered by some to be too hard-edged and unfeminine with the 'bumps of mathematics … too strongly marked'! After her death, Somerville College in the University of Oxford was named in her honour.

Bronze medallion,
14.3 diameter
Bought in 1991
PG 2847

John Gibson Lockhart 1794–1854 and Sophia Scott 1799–1837
by Robert Scott Lauder

Oil on canvas,
76.8 × 64.8
Bought in 1985
PG 2672

In 1818, through their mutual admiration for Goethe, the young essayist and reviewer, John Gibson Lockhart, met Walter Scott and they became firm friends. Two years later Lockhart married Scott's eldest daughter, Sophia, and they settled in a cottage on Scott's estate at Abbotsford in the Borders.

This portrait appears to have been painted to commemorate that marriage. But Robert Scott Lauder was only seventeen at the time of the wedding and had hardly started his career. It is likely that this double portrait was painted around 1840, after Sophia's death in 1837 and Scott Lauder's return to Britain from Italy a year later. If this, then, is a commemorative portrait, commissioned by a young widower, it would explain Sophia's dominance in the picture, the prominence of her wedding ring and the veil she holds in her hand.

The Lockharts' happy family life was a great support to Sir Walter Scott, particularly after his financial crash in 1826. Lockhart's The Life of Sir Walter Scott was published between 1836 and 1838, and all the profits from the work were paid to Scott's creditors.

The Reverend Thomas Chalmers 1780–1847 by Augustin Edouart

The man who led the Disruption movement of 1843, when 470 Church of Scotland ministers resigned their livings and broke away to form the Free Church, was more fascinated by mathematics than theology as a boy, and as a young minister had been attracted by both materialism and atheism. His deep and sincere evangelism came later, partly from studies, but mostly resulting from his experiences in Glasgow, where the degradation of the urban poor prompted both practical action (encouraging the building of new churches and better management of pauperism) and spiritual reflection. His work as an active social reformer among the 'home heathens' was balanced by periods spent in academia, at both the universities of St Andrews and Edinburgh, and latterly, as Principal of the New College of the Free Church.

Chalmers was renowned as a moving orator, not because of the words themselves or any beauty of voice, but because of the intensity of his delivery. 'How he burns!' one witness commented, 'I shed more tears of genuine imagination than I have done since they were forced from me by the magnificence of Mrs Siddons'. An American visitor described how Chalmers 'throws himself forward as if he would pitch headlong out of the pulpit'.

Silhouette on watercolour background, 27.6 × 18.7
Bought in 1933
PG 1211

The Reverend Thomas Guthrie 1803–1873 by James Edgar

Oil on millboard,
54·7 × 45·7
Dated 1862
Bought in 1984
PG 2633

Thomas Guthrie was the leading churchman and social reformer of his day. He helped to found the Free Church of Scotland in 1843 and it is in the shadow of his Free St John's Church, at the head of Edinburgh's Lawnmarket, that James Edgar has portrayed him. In the distance is St Giles Cathedral. Though these two buildings allude to Guthrie's role as a great churchman, it is his work as a social reformer that is the main subject of this painting. Thomas Guthrie stands among the ragged children of Edinburgh's slums. He was a vehement advocate of education for all children, the poor as well as the rich. At the right of the picture men and women are shown standing in a tavern. Guthrie was also a powerful supporter of the temperance movement, well aware that many of Scotland's social problems were related to the abuse of alcohol.

Edgar's portrait of Guthrie has similarities with William Scott's portrait of the missionary Robert Moffat. The urban poor of Britain were, in some quarters, thought to be in just as much need of a civilising mission as the peoples of Africa and Asia.

David Livingstone 1813–1873 by Thomas Annan

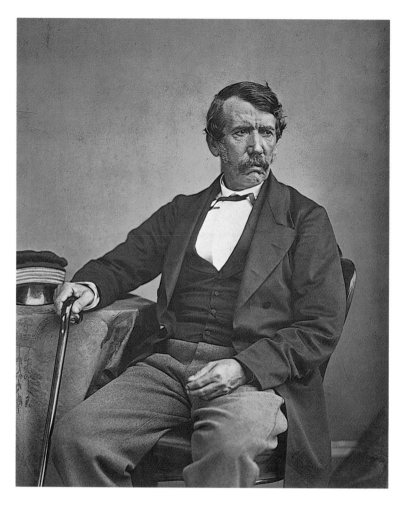

Photograph, 36.8 × 30.1
Acquired by the Gallery at
an unknown date
PGP 74.2

David Livingstone was the most influential and unorthodox missionary of the nineteenth century. He devoted his life to the eradication of the slave trade in Africa and aimed to promote both commerce and Christianity as the pioneering influences of civilisation. His journey from coast to coast, discovering the Victoria Falls, made him a national hero, much lionised on his return to Britain in 1856. His next major expedition, to the Zambesi from 1858 to 1864, was sponsored by the British government.

This photograph was taken in Hamilton in 1864 when Livingstone was visiting his sisters who lived next door to the photographer. This is the most successful portrait of Livingstone, who did not enjoy having his picture taken. The cap on the table is of particular significance as his 'Consul's cap', symbolising his authority as a roving consul in the Zambesi expedition.

Robert Moffat 1795–1883 with John Mokoteri and Sarah Roby
by William Scott

Oil on canvas, 53.4 × 45.7
Dated 1842
Bought in 1964
PG 2035

Born in East Lothian and trained as a gardener, Robert Moffat turned to mission work and was sent to Africa by the London Missionary Society. He arrived in Cape Town in 1817 and eventually established the Kuruman Mission in Bechuanaland, which still survives. This portrait was painted on a rare visit back to Britain. It shows Moffat, Bible in hand – he had translated the New Testament into the Sechwana language – preaching in the company of two young Africans, Sarah Roby and John Mokoteri. Sarah was found abandoned and John was rescued after the battle of Lattakoo.

They were adopted by Robert Moffat and his wife Mary, and they travelled with them to Britain.

Robert and Mary Moffat's eldest daughter Mary married another great African missionary and explorer, David Livingstone, in 1844.

Thomas Carlyle 1795–1881 *by Walter Greaves*

Oil on panel, 62.9 × 40.6
Gifted by Arthur Kay in
1925
PG 982

French Revolution (1837), *Cromwell's Letters* (1845), and *Frederick the Great* (1858–65). Carlyle married the beautiful and brilliant Jane Baillie Welsh (1801–1866) in 1826. Theirs was a marriage in which they both loved and frustrated one another, she fiercely protective of him but her own genius unfulfilled and overpowered by his. Their childlessness was also a source of enduring pain to them both and they were increasingly tormented by illness, real or neurotically induced. Most of their married life was spent in London where their house in Cheyne Walk became a place of pilgrimage for other intellectuals from all over Europe.

There are numerous portraits of Thomas Carlyle, the most famous of which is James McNeil Whistler's *Arrangement in Grey and Black No.2* (Glasgow Art Gallery). Walter Greaves was a protégé of Whistler and another of Carlyle's neighbours in Chelsea. Greaves made studies for this portrait while Carlyle was sitting for Whistler in 1879. Carlyle was an advocate of the idea of the portrait gallery as a pantheon, and his influence led to the founding of the National Portrait Gallery in London in 1856, and subsequently, after his death, to the creation of a Scottish National Portrait Gallery in 1889.

The historian and essayist Thomas Carlyle was one of the most prolific and influential writers of the nineteenth century. Born in Ecclefechan, the son of a stone-mason, it was his father's intention that he should be trained for the ministry. He consequently received a classical education and studied at the University of Edinburgh. Although Carlyle abandoned orthodox religious beliefs, his subsequent writings were to be imbued with the spirit of Scottish Calvinism. His writings include *A Life of Schiller* (1825), *Sartor Resartus* (1833–4), *The*

David Laing 1793–1878 by Sir William Fettes Douglas

No artist more suitable could have been chosen to paint an antiquary engrossed in his research and surrounded by his papers and collection than Sir William Fettes Douglas. He made a career of painting scenes of this sort, generally choosing subjects from history or fiction, but in David Laing he was able to paint a contemporary who could rival an antiquary or bibliophile of any age.

In 1819 Laing, then a young Edinburgh bookseller, visited Copenhagen to meet the great Icelandic scholar Grímur Thorkelin. He bought two thousand items from Thorkelin's library and later sold them to the Faculty of Advocates in Edinburgh. They now form an important collection within the National Library of Scotland. When Sir Walter Scott founded the Bannatyne Club in 1823, to publish unedited material relating to the history and literature of Scotland, he chose Laing to become the club's secretary and chief organ-

iser. Laing was also the librarian of the Signet Library in Edinburgh for over forty years.

This portrait was painted in 1862 as a gift from the artist to the Royal Scottish Academy where Laing was honorary Professor of Antiquities. His great and numerous collection of Old Master drawings is the foundation of the National Gallery of Scotland's collection. His important manuscripts were bequeathed to the University of Edinburgh.

Oil on canvas, 25.5 × 63.5
Transferred from the National Gallery of Scotland in 1964
PG 2041

Hugh Miller 1802–1856 by David Octavius Hill and Robert Adamson

High Miller was an extraordinary man. He began his working life as a mason, turned to the carving of churchyard monuments, tried writing poetry and eventually settled for prose, and even worked as a banker. In his spare time he investigated Scotland's impressive geology and he became a fluent, best-selling writer on the subject. From 1840, he was the editor of *The Witness* newspaper. He was one of the first to pose for Hill and Adamson and one of the first to write a critical article on the possibilities of photography, in the months of June and July 1843.

In this photograph taken in the same year, Miller is shown as a stone mason, as he had been in earlier life. He wrote that the itinerant sculptor was the model of a modern philosopher or hermit – acquainted at first hand with the past lives and grief of strangers. Ironically, he had met his future wife while working in a graveyard and his last monumental work had been the gravestone of his little daughter. Posing for this picture would have been, therefore, an intensely serious and reflective undertaking – revealing the inner life of the journalist who, he said, 'writes on the sand when the flood is coming in.'

Calotype photograph,
15.2 × 11
Bequeathed from the Elliot
Collection in 1950
PGP HA 281

James Nasmyth 1808–1890 by David Octavius Hill and Robert Adamson

Calotype photograph,
19.9 × 15.2
Acquired by the Gallery at
an unknown date
PGP HA 541

James Nasmyth, the son of the painter Alexander Nasmyth, was a close friend of D.O. Hill. He was an engineer and invented the steam hammer and pile driver, which revolutionised industry and engineering work throughout the world, from the docks of Glasgow to Russia and the Nile. He was greatly interested in the invention of photography, which he described as 'a delightful means of educating the eye for artistic feeling, as well as educating the hands in delicate manipulation.' This particular photograph was also the cause of a remarkable meeting. A Glasgow engraver, Andrew Maclure, was travelling through England with a copy in his portmanteau which enabled him to recognise Nasmyth at a railway station and they were thus able to strike up a friendship.

Elizabeth Johnstone Hall by David Octavius Hill and Robert Adamson

Calotype photograph,
19.5 × 15
Gifted by the Edinburgh
Photographic Society in
1987
PGP EPS 69

Elizabeth Johnstone Hall was a Newhaven fishwife. While their husbands faced the worst dangers of fishing in the North Sea, the wives were responsible for most of the transactions on land. They prepared and brought the catch up from the shores of the Forth into Edinburgh, where they sold it in the market and to individual housewives. They carried the one or two hundredweight of fish in creels on their backs two miles, substantially uphill, and often returned later in the day with a similar load of oysters. The fishwives were noted for their commercial skill and confidence and also for their distinctive striped dress. They were often strikingly beautiful, with clear singing voices.

This photograph is composed with a particular loving care for the stripes and folds of the dress, and the shadowed wicker of the basket. Hill captioned the photograph 'A Newhaven beauty: "It's not fish you're buying, it's men's lives."'

Willie Liston by David Octavius Hill and Robert Adamson

Calotype photograph,
19.4 × 13.8
Gifted by the Edinburgh
Photographic Society in
1987
PGP EPS 73

Willie Liston was a fisherman working from the village of Newhaven on the shores of the River Forth, to the north of Edinburgh. The Newhaven fishermen had a well-earned reputation for skill and courage. They fished from small open boats, both close to land and some miles out and well up the north-east coast – principally for herring, haddock and cod. They also dredged for oysters in the Forth. Liston is here shown 'redding', or preparing the line. The line for inshore fishing, usually baited with mussels, could carry from 500 to 3,000 hooks and the catch was often phenomenally large. When they followed the herring shoals up the coast to the town of Wick in 1840, 900 boats brought in more than 48,000 fish for salting and export. In the 1840s, when this photograph was taken, the life was certainly hard, but it was still possible to make a good living fishing all year round.

William Dyce 1806–1864 by David Scott

The painter William Dyce was born in Aberdeen. He was educated at Marischal College where his father lectured in medicine. After training briefly at the Royal Academy schools in London, Dyce made the first of three visits to Italy. The study of early Italian painting and the art of Raphael were to be the formative influences on his own developing style. This drawing of Dyce in a gondola sketching out of doors was done on his third visit to Italy in 1832 by his friend David Scott. It was in Italy that Dyce encountered the German Nazarene painters whose emulation of the Italian primitives was also to influence him. He returned to Scotland and during the 1830s painted a number of portraits. In 1837 he exhibited a painting in the Nazarene manner, a Dantesque subject, *Paolo and Francesca*. He subsequently painted several versions of the Madonna and Child which directly emulated the style of Raphael. Dyce also revived the techniques of the early Italians. He was commissioned by Prince Albert to paint a fresco at Osborne House on the Isle of Wight and was encouraged by him to submit designs for frescoes for the Houses of Parliament. Dyce became Director of the School of Design in London in 1840 and in 1844 published his *Theory of the Fine Arts*. In the 1850s, Dyce became associated with the pre-Raphaelite 'brotherhood' (D.G. Rossetti, J.E. Millais and Holman Hunt). Dyce influenced, and was influenced by, these younger artists. His late paintings are characterised by the same dedicated observation and minute recording of natural detail that typifies pre-Raphaelitism. His masterpiece, *Pegwell Bay: A Recollection of October 5, 1858* (Tate Gallery), painted in 1859/60 is remarkable for its intense verisimilitude.

Watercolour on paper,
24.2 × 22.8
Dated 1832
Gifted by William Bell Scott
in 1887
PG 208

Sir Alexander Morison 1779–1866 by Richard Dadd

Alexander Morison was one of the pioneers of psychiatric medicine and a leading authority on mental diseases. He was born in Edinburgh and was apprenticed to a surgeon, but, after marrying a rich wife, contemplated giving up medicine altogether to concentrate his energies on managing her estates.

Through the intervention of some London friends, Morison was appointed visiting physician to the private lunatic asylums of Surrey. A visit to Paris where he met Esquirol, the most influential French psychiatrist of his day, determined the rest of Morison's life.

This portrait was painted at the end of Morison's seventeen years as consultant to Bethlem Asylum in Southwark. Its exceptional interest lies in the fact that it was painted by one of his patients, Richard Dadd.

Dadd was a well-known artist but began to suffer from delusional misidentification. He murdered his father believing him to be the devil. The background of Dadd's portrait, almost certainly a commission, shows the doctor's estate at Anchorfield on the Firth of Forth at Newhaven. This was taken from a sketch provided by Morison's daughter. The fishwives were probably based on photographs taken by Hill and Adamson.

Oil on canvas, 51.1 × 61.3
Dated 1852
Bought with help from the National Heritage Memorial Fund in 1984
PG 2623

Elizabeth Rigby, Lady Eastlake 1809–1893 by David Octavius Hill and Robert Adamson

Calotype photograph,
20.7 × 15.1
Bequeathed from the Elliot
Collection in 1950
PGP HA 286

Elizabeth Rigby was a journalist and art critic, writing in an acid and witty manner for such journals as the *Quarterly Review*. She was one of the earliest enthusiasts for photography and posed more than twenty times for Hill and Adamson. In a review of their work in 1846, she referred to 'the beautiful and wonderful Calotype drawings – so precious in every real artist's sight, not only for their own matchless truth of Nature, but as the triumphant proof of all to be most revered as truth in art.' This photograph also reflects her interest in costume and the aesthetic effects of women's dress – here the graceful drape of a Paisley shawl. She later married the painter and director of the National Gallery in London, Sir Charles Eastlake.

Isabella Burns Begg 1771–1858 by David Octavius Hill and Robert Adamson

Isabella Burns Begg was the youngest sister of the poet, Robert Burns. She had a hard life, was widowed young and left with the rearing of nine children. She kept her family by setting up a village school. In later years, she was allowed a picturesque cottage where she lived almost as a monument to her brother, entertaining 'hundreds upon hundreds from every corner of the United Kingdom and from the Continent and America.' Her obituary remarks: 'Hers was the natural manner which art cannot communicate and which is beyond convention.'

Hill was a great admirer of Burns and had published a large set of landscape paintings as *The Land of Burns*. Hill was familiar with the painted portrait of Burns and would have been much struck with the resemblance between the poet and his sister. Robert Burns died before photography was established – but here, through this strongly expressed portrait of a woman, we can, astonishingly, grasp an idea of how the man might have looked in old age.

Calotype photograph,
20 × 13.8
Acquired by the Gallery at
an unknown date
PGP HA 277

Sir James Hope Grant 1808–1875 by *Felice Beato*

James Hope Grant was a professional soldier who served in most of the major campaigns in China and India of his day. Between 1839 and 1842 he fought in the Opium War when the British took possession of Hong Kong. This photograph was taken during the 1860 campaign when he led a combined French and British force to 'encourage' the Emperor of China to recognise his European trading treaties. Felice Beato arrived in China for the taking of Peking (Beijing) and set up an impromptu studio, photographing the general with the mud of the battlefield still on his boots.

Grant also fought with considerable distinction in India during the campaigns against the Sikhs, which resulted in the annexation of the Punjab in 1849. He resisted the Indian Mutiny and eventually assumed command of the Madras army. Lord Clyde thought highly of his abilities: 'Hope has a clear head for business and a sound judgement; and as to handling troops in the field, he is quite perfection.'

Albumen photograph,
16.9 × 13.2
Bought in 1938
PGP 19.1

Sir Colin Campbell, Lord Clyde 1792–1863 by Thomas Jones Barker

Oil on millboard,
62.2 × 45.1
Gifted by the Earl of
Rosebery in 1890
PG 284

Colin Campbell was the son of a Glasgow carpenter. He joined the army at the age of sixteen and fought bravely in the Napoleonic wars. Promotion, however, was slow to come. During the Crimean War he commanded the Highland Brigade and, at the battle of Balaclava, formed part of the famous 'thin red line'. Campbell's fierce attachment to his Highlanders earned him accusations of favouritism.

In 1857 Lord Palmerston offered Campbell supreme command in India to quell the Mutiny. He sailed within twenty-four hours and was responsible for the second relief of Lucknow. At the storming of Secunderabad, after the failure of the first attack, he called out to one of his colonels, 'bring on the tartan – let my own lads at them.'

Campbell left India in 1859, having gained a peerage and the thanks of Parliament.

Queen Victoria 1819–1901

The Baptism of Prince Maurice of Battenberg at Balmoral
by George Ogilvy Reid
Oil on canvas, 23.7 × 35.6
Dated 1891
Bought in 1936
PG 1306

Queen Victoria and her consort, Prince Albert, visited Scotland for the first time in the summer of 1842 – this was only the second visit to the country by a reigning British monarch since the Act of Union. They fell passionately in love with Scotland and established a new tradition of annual royal residence, renting, and then buying, the Balmoral estate on Deeside. Balmoral Castle, constructed from 1852, remains to this day a living symbol of the royal family's attachment to Scotland.

Alexander Brodie received sittings from Queen Victoria at Balmoral in 1865 and 1866 for a statue (now at Aberdeen City Chambers) and a portrait bust. The queen was particularly concerned that the results should be distinctly Scottish – in the statue she wears a tartan plaid fastened by a thistle brooch, while in the bust, the thistle takes its place alongside the English rose and Irish clover leaf as emblems decorating the neckline of

her dress. Brodie's quest for perfection in this commission is thought to have been a contributory factor in his suicide, at the age of thirty-seven, in 1867. William, his elder brother, finished the bust.

The painting, a sketch for a picture commissioned by Queen Victoria, shows the christening at Balmoral of the queen's grandson, Prince Maurice, on 31 October 1891. The old queen holds the baby while Dr Rees, the local minister, pronounces his blessing. It was the first baptism of a royal prince in Scotland for three hundred years, a historic occasion which the queen fully appreciated.

OPPOSITE
Queen Victoria
by Alexander and William Brodie
Marble bust, 67.7 high
Transferred from the National Gallery of Scotland in 1936
PG 1068

138

Professor Sir Henry Littlejohn 1828–1914 *by Sir George Reid*

Henry Littlejohn was responsible for slum clearance in Edinburgh and for educating its citizens in cleanliness and sanitation. He trained in medicine at the University of Edinburgh where he became a lecturer and later Professor of Medical Jurisprudence. In 1862 he was to gain much greater influence with his appointment as Edinburgh's first medical officer of health. The death rate in the city was dramatically reduced during his term. As a teacher, he was noted for his dramatic power and for the fascination which he exerted on his class, often numbering over 250 students. This portrait, which captures the authority and determination of the man, was presented to him by his pupils on his retiral in 1907.

Oil on canvas,
102.2 × 76.2
Bequeathed by Professor
Harvey Littlejohn in 1927
PG 1042

Sir James Young Simpson 1811–1870 by John Stevenson Rhind from the plaster by Patric Park

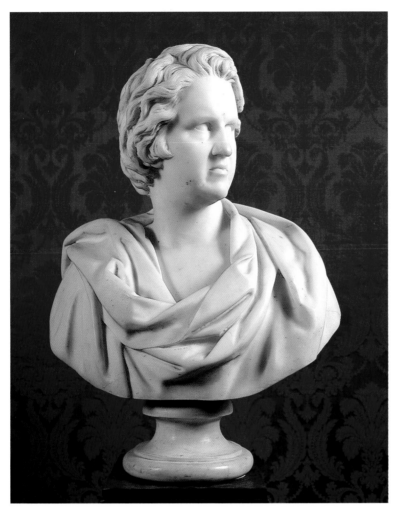

Marble bust, 79.5 high
Gifted by Sir W.G. Simpson
in 1889
PG 426

James Young Simpson was the seventh son of the village baker in Bathgate. His family all supported his time at the University of Edinburgh and he graduated in medicine in 1832. His ability was recognised early and he was made Professor of Midwifery at the age of twenty-eight. His interest in the use of anaesthetics in childbirth led him to try sulphuric ether and, in 1847, he and two colleagues tried inhaling chloroform. Its usefulness was demonstrated publicly a fortnight later at the Edinburgh Infirmary. Despite disconcerting opposition, principally on the religious grounds that 'man was born to suffering,' chloroform came into general use and was endorsed by Queen Victoria. Simpson's achievements in obstetrics and gynaecology were considerable and his interests lay 'as far asunder as acupressure and the use of the pyramids.'

Patric Park's head is a monumental rendering of an inspiring and vigorous personality.

Samuel Smiles 1812–1904 by Sir George Reid

Oil on canvas, 34.3 × 24.8
Dated 1891
Bequeathed by John Miller
Gray in 1894
PG 631

Samuel Smiles studied medicine at Edinburgh and practised as a doctor in his native Haddington. He later moved to Leeds as a surgeon. However, he abandoned his medical career for journalism, becoming editor of the *Leeds Times*. He also became involved in the management of railways. While in Leeds he met George Stephenson, the inventor and founder of railways. He wrote his biography and followed it with further lives of George Moore, James Nasmyth and Josiah Wedgwood. By far his most popular book is *Self-Help*, published in 1859. A collection of brief lives of great achievers, it became a standard school prize in Victorian Britain.

William Ewart Gladstone 1809–1898 by Franz von Lenbach

Gladstone was born in Liverpool of Scottish parents. He was educated at Eton and Oxford, where he proved to be an outstanding classical scholar. Gladstone went on to study law but was never called to the bar. He was elected to Parliament in 1832, as member for Midlothian, and was to become leader of the Liberal Party, serving four terms as Prime Minister and five times as Chancellor of the Exchequer, twice holding both offices together. He was one of the greatest parliamentarians of the nineteenth century. While in office, he had to face a succession of troubles in Ireland, the Sudan and South Africa. At the same time he succeeded in introducing electoral reforms which, together with those introduced by his rival, Disraeli, came near to creating universal suffrage. (Neither went so far as to extend the vote to women.) Gladstone was also prolific as an author, his works included studies of Homer and translations of Horace.

The Bavarian artist, Franz von Lenbach, depicts Gladstone as an elder statesman in an image that expresses sombre concentration and stern integrity.

Oil on canvas,
108.6 × 86.4
Bought in 1914
PG 837

Thomas Stevenson 1818–1887 by Sir George Reid

Thomas was the youngest son of Robert Stevenson (1722–1850), lighthouse engineer and designer of the famous Bell Rock lighthouse on the Inchcape Rock. As partners in the family firm he and his two brothers, Alan and David, were all successively employed by the Northern Lighthouse Board and acted as consulting engineers to the lighthouse boards of India, New Zealand and Japan. His greatest achievement was the designing of a revolving light, a modified form of Fresnel's fixed light apparatus.

His inventions won him an international reputation. In 1885 he was elected President of the Royal Society of Edinburgh, and, as one of the original members of the Scottish Meteorological Society, he was particularly active in establishing the high-level observatory on Ben Nevis.

By his wife, Margaret Balfour, daughter of the minister of Colinton, he was the father of Robert Louis Stevenson, who paid a moving tribute to him in *Memoirs and Portraits*.

Oil on canvas, 86.3 × 63.5
Bequeathed by Mrs Thomas
Stevenson in 1897
PG 568

William Thomson, Lord Kelvin 1824–1907 by T. and R. Annan and Sons

William Thomson arrived in Glasgow from Belfast at the age of eight. By the time he was eleven, he was able to join the university as a student. There, and at the universities of Cambridge and Paris, he made his mark in mathematical physics. At the age of twenty-one he had published twelve original papers and at twenty-two was appointed Professor of Natural Philosophy in Glasgow where he set up the first physics laboratory in Great Britain and proved an inspiring teacher.

Throughout his life, Thomson worked on the problems of thermodynamics and electricity. His pure researches were tied to practical uses and one of his public achievements was the supervision and correction of faults in the laying of the Atlantic telegraph cable between 1857 and 1866. He linked a number of his investigations and inventions to his own pleasure in sailing and succeeded, for example, in devising a method of taking soundings while a ship was in movement which he used to navigate in fog. With James White, a Glasgow optician, he established a firm to make measuring instruments from his own patents, such as galvanometers and standard electrical balances. In the photograph, taken by the Glasgow firm of T. & R. Annan, Thomson is shown resting on a binnacle holding a marine azimuth mirror.

Helmholtz, who worked in the same field and was a close friend of Thomson, said when they first met: 'He far exceeds all the great men of science with whom I have made personal acquaintance, in intelligence and lucidity, and mobility of thought.' Thirty years later he added, '... he was full of speculations, and as you know, he will not stop for meals or any other consideration.'

Carbon photograph, 19 × 14.7
Bought in 1933
PGP 230.1

James Grieve 1841–1924 by Henry Wright Kerr

James Grieve was an important horticulturist and a prominent character within Edinburgh's botanical set. Born in Peebles, he was apprenticed at the age of twelve to a local nursery and spent four years working in the gardens of Stobo Castle. In 1859 Grieve moved to Edinburgh, then considered a 'Mecca for young gardeners', and was employed as nursery manager for Dickson and Company at their Leith Walk premises. He subsequently began his own family business with his two sons. Grieve became well known for his successful hybridisation of many flowers, particularly violas, pinks and carnations. In 1870, his display of new pansies at Crystal Palace caused a furore when critics condemned his exhibits as 'weeds', but his hybrids soon became the fashionable norm. He raised several hybrid rhododendrons, including the *Rhododendron grievei* and produced a number of new apples, the most popular being the dessert apple 'James Grieve', which was particularly suited to the Scottish climate.

Watercolour, 79.4 × 56.5
Gifted by Ian Scott in 1962
PG 1990

Andrew Lang 1844–1912 by Sir William Blake Richmond

Oil on canvas, 111.8 × 86.3
Bequeathed by Mrs Andrew
Lang in 1933
PG 1206

Lang's versatility as a writer – he was, among other things, a poet, an art critic, a historian, a Homeric scholar and an anthropologist – convinced some contemporaries that 'Andrew Lang' must be the common pen-name of a whole group of scholars.

A distant cousin and close friend of Robert Louis Stevenson, he is often mistaken for him. Their similarity in appearance is, however, probably more to do with the fashions of the time and the type of image men in their milieu wished to project.

Lang's *Blue Fairy Book* (1889) and *Red Fairy Book* (1890) did much to revive the popularity of fairy-tales. His verse *Ballades in Blue China*, published in 1880, reflected the contemporary fascination with Japanese art, also an interest of the group of painters known as the 'Glasgow Boys'.

Charles Rennie Mackintosh 1868–1928 by Francis Henry Newbery

Oil on canvas,
110. 5 × 61.4
Bought in 1933
PG 1205

The architect, watercolour painter and designer Charles Rennie Mackintosh was born in Glasgow, the son of a police superintendent. After leaving Glasgow School of Art he served an apprenticeship with the Glasgow architect, John Hutcheson, before joining the firm of Honeyman and Keppie in 1889. In 1897 he won the commission for his firm to design new premises for the School of Art in Renfrew Street. He owed this remark-able commission to the imaginative patronage of the School's director, Fra Newbery. Newbery's portrait of the architect shows him with his plans for the School of Art in his hands.

Mackintosh was the leading exponent of the art nouveau style in Scotland and his influence on the other artists and craftsmen working in the 'Glasgow style' was significant. He married Margaret Macdonald in 1900 and they often collaborated on commissions. Mackintosh exhibited at the Vienna Secession exhibition in 1900, where his work met with critical acclaim. By 1914, however, he was to leave Scotland with a sense of disap-pointment and the belief that his work was not valued in his native country. He carried out some highly original architectural work in Northampton and produced textile designs to eke out a living. He subsequently lived in France until 1927, during which time he painted a series of extraordinary watercolours. He died in London in 1928.

Sir Robert Lorimer 1864–1929 by John Henry Lorimer

This informal portrait of the young Robert Lorimer at his architectural studies was painted by his elder brother John. Robert was then being trained by Robert Rowand Anderson whose major project at the time was the construction of the Scottish National Portrait Gallery.

Lorimer rapidly earned a reputation for his arts and crafts cottages, his sensitive country house restorations and his garden designs. By 1911 he was acknowledged as Scotland's leading architect. That was the year he received a knighthood for his designs for the Thistle Chapel at St Giles. Sir Robert's career was crowned with the popular and professional success of the Scottish National War Memorial (1924–27), converted from a disused barracks within Edinburgh Castle.

Throughout his career he worked closely with craftsmen – plasterers, iron-workers, sculptors, carvers and stained-glass artists. For the Scottish National War Memorial his team was seventy strong.

Oil on canvas, 25.4 × 35.5
Dated 1886
Gifted by the Royal Institute of British Architects in 1938
PG 1353

Robert Louis Stevenson 1850–1894 by Count Girolamo Nerli

Oil on canvas, 61 × 35.5
Bequeathed by Mrs Turnbull in 1915
PG 847

Born in Edinburgh, Robert Louis Stevenson was an unhealthy, if energetic, child and received an eccentric education while travelling in Britain and Europe. He proved unequal to his father's profession of engineering and qualified in law in 1875, but by this time he had already turned to writing and had begun his remarkable essays on life and literature.

In 1876 he met Mrs Fanny Osbourne, an American whom he married in California in 1880 after she had obtained a divorce. She proved a perfect match, supporting him in his writing and nursing him in ill-health – his chronic lung disease was by now apparent. Nevertheless, he completed *Treasure Island* in 1882 and *The Black Arrow* in 1883, when he also began *The Child's Garden of Verses*. In 1886 he achieved popular and commercial success with two books, *The Strange Case of Dr Jekyll and Mr Hyde* and *Kidnapped*. In 1887 he moved to the United States, where he wrote *The Master of Ballantrae*. His family then set out on a sea voyage, eventually settling on Samoa. His prolific output finished only with his death and the uncompleted books of *St Ives* and *Weir of Hermiston*.

Girolamo Nerli became a friend of Stevenson on Samoa and there attempted this difficult, restless sitter. Mrs Stevenson remarked that, 'With such a sitter, the victim is the artist', but Stevenson himself was pleased with the result.

Sir James Matthew Barrie 1860–1937 by Sir William Nicholson

Born at Kirriemuir in Angus, J. M. Barrie is best know today for his creation of Peter Pan, 'the boy who never grew up'. A small man, his complex adult life stemmed from an ambivalent attitude to childhood and the problems of leaving the world of boyhood behind.

Barrie produced a series of autobiographical novels, including The Window in Thrums and The Little Minister, before writing various successful plays. Among these were The Admirable Crichton (1902), Dear Brutus (1917), Mary Rose (1920) and The Boy David (1936).

William Nicholson was designing costumes for the first stage production of Peter Pan in 1904, when it was suggested that Barrie should sit for his portrait between rehearsals. To this Barrie agreed, although he said in a letter, 'I have long ceased to be on speaking terms with my face, so why have it painted?' The composition, in which the subject seems anxious to evade our attention, hints at the essential loneliness of Barrie.

Oil on canvas, 58.4 × 52.7
Dated 1904
Bought with help from the National Art
Collections Fund in 1943
PG 1438

Duncan Grant 1885–1978 · *Self-portrait in a mirror*

Duncan Grant visited Matisse in Paris in 1911 and watched him at work on a number of large canvases, including the great *La Danse*. Initially, he found the French artist's work confusing, unlike anything he had previously experienced. But, in a short while, he moved in the same direction himself, creating his own version of rhythmic post-impressionism.

Grant was a prominent member of the literary and artistic circle, the Bloomsbury group, which included the writer Virginia Woolf, the art critic Clive Bell and the economist Maynard Keynes who was Grant's lover for several years. In the background of this self-portrait, reversed in the mirror, Grant has included Matisse's *Woman Seated in an Arm Chair*. When it was exhibited for sale in London in 1919, Duncan Grant persuaded Keynes to buy it.

Oil on canvas, 61 × 45.8
Bought in 1980
PG 2459

Joseph Crawhall 1861–1913 by Edward Arthur Walton

The artist Joseph Crawhall is shown in a studio standing against the back of a canvas which itself is propped against another, depicting a bull fight. Bull fighting posters and the inscription 'Madrid 84' indicate several of the pre-occupations of Crawhall's artistic life: animals, Spain and Spanish North Africa.

Crawhall and Walton, who were related through the marriage of Crawhall's sister to Walton's brother, were two of the leading artists of the radical group, the 'Glasgow Boys'. Their work shocked the conservative artistic establishment. The President of the Royal Scottish Academy, Sir George Reid, for one, poured scorn on the young artists, complaining that 'the so-called Impressionists have, unfortunately, some followers in Scotland. There is quite a school of them in Glasgow ... I greatly dislike young artists going in for this kind of thing. It is simply an impertinence.' The reaction of the 'Glasgow Boys' can be seen by the way they responded to such criticism. Prominently inscribed on this canvas are the words: 'Joe Crawhall the impressionist by E.A. Walton the realist'.

Oil on canvas, 74.3 × 36.8
Dated 1884
Gifted by Mrs E.A. Walton in 1924
PG 971

James Craig Annan 1864–1946 by William Strang

Chalk and watercolour on paper,
32.2 × 20.1
Dated 1902
Bought in 1972
PG 2205

J. Craig Annan was the son of the Glasgow photographer, Thomas Annan, and joined his brother, Tom, in the family firm. In 1883 he travelled to Vienna with his father to learn the photogravure process from the inventor, Karl Klic, and purchased the rights to use the process in Great Britain and Ireland.

Annan was a trained chemist and learnt his art from the company of painters, the example of his father and the work of David Octavius Hill and Robert Adamson. Working principally in photogravure and platinum printing, he produced personal work of great subtlety and variety between the 1890s and 1920s. He was a member of the Linked Ring group of photographers and exhibited his work internationally. He had a particular influence on North American photography through Alfred Stieglitz who published his and Hill and Adamson's photographs in the critically important journal, *Camera Work*.

Annan had a reputation among his fellow photographers as a 'natural' photographer and wrote: 'I never followed a pre-determined path in my work. I just did what seemed to be the most beautiful and most natural thing at that moment.' He adopted the Latin motto, 'Ars est celare artem' – art conceals its skill. His friend, William Strang, has drawn him in the tradition of Holbein's naturalism, a kind of delicate and direct portraiture appropriate to a man concerned with nature.

Jessie Marion King 1875–1949 by James Craig Annan

Jessie M. King was one of the outstanding designers trained in Glasgow at the turn of the last century. She studied at Glasgow School of Art and from 1895 to 1899 won a scholarship to visit Italy and Germany. She quickly became famous internationally as a book illustrator and also produced designs for jewellery and wallpaper.

In 1902 Jessie M. King collaborated with Charles Rennie Mackintosh on the Scottish Pavilion at the Esposizione Nazionale in Turin, where she won a gold medal. With her husband, the furniture designer E.A. Taylor, King moved to Paris in 1910 but returned to Scotland at the outbreak of war and settled in Kirkcudbright, which by then was an artists' colony.

Autochrome photograph, 16.4 × 12
Acquired by the Gallery at an unknown date
PGP 96.1

Douglas Haig, 1st Earl Haig 1861–1928 by John Singer Sargent

Douglas Haig was a professional soldier who first saw active service in the reconquest of Sudan in 1897. He took part in the Boer War and achieved independent command in 1900. In 1906 he became a director in the War Office, helping to define the principles of military organisation and tactics later employed in the First World War. He then became commander-in-chief in India.

From the outbreak of the European war, he was engaged in the desperate and bloody trench warfare. In 1915 he was given command of the First Army and at the end of the year succeeded Sir John French as commander-in-chief of the British armies. The long and lethal struggle for ground, fought in his phrase 'with our backs to the wall', only ended with the breaking of the Hindenburg lines in October 1918.

After the war, Haig was responsible for uniting the ex-servicemen in the Royal British Legion and worked for the combined United Services Fund and Royal British Legion to the benefit of servicemen and their dependents.

Oil on canvas, 56 × 41
Bought in 1925
PG 1010

Dr Elsie Maud Inglis 1864–1917 by Ivan Mestrovic

Dr Inglis was one of the first women to study medicine at Edinburgh and Glasgow and, once qualified, devoted herself to ameliorating the treatment of her sex. In Edinburgh she established a maternity hospital staffed entirely by women (inspired by her time with Dr Garrett Anderson in London) and played a major role in starting up a second medical school for women. Inglis, not least because of her experiences in the medical profession, was an active supporter of the fight for women's suffrage and was a founder member of the Scottish Women's Suffragette Federation.

When the First World War broke out Inglis had the idea of establishing all-women units of doctors, nurses and orderlies to set up field-hospitals. The War Office turned her offer down but France and Serbia accepted, and the Scottish Women's Hospitals for Foreign Service came into being, staffed by volunteers and funded by donations. Initially Inglis remained in Britain organising the units, but in 1915 she went to Serbia to relieve a colleague. Serbia was soon overrun but Inglis stayed at her hospital, winning the admiration of the Serbs and eventually being captured. Repatriated in 1917, she soon returned to assist the Serbs on the Balkan front, leaving only when they were finally ordered out of Russia. Inglis died the day after her boat docked at Newcastle.

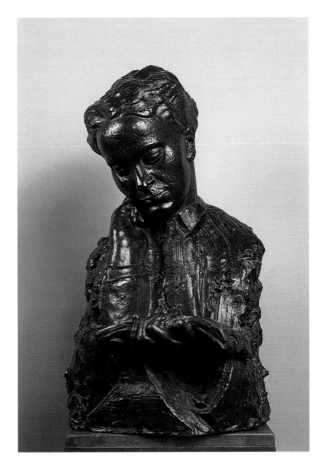

Bronze bust, 66 high
Modelled in 1918
Gifted by the people of Serbia in 1918
PG 1825

Sir Harry Lauder 1870–1950 by Henry Mayo Bateman

Pencil, ink and watercolour on paper, 29.1 × 30.2
Dated 1915
Bought in 1972
PG 2202

One of the most successful and best loved stars of the music-hall, Lauder's popularity stretched across the English-speaking world and many of his songs are still familiar today. When Lauder was eleven his father died and he worked in an Arbroath flax-mill as a 'half-timer' to support the family. By thirteen he was in the pits in Hamilton but he became well-known for his fine singing voice, winning prizes at local music competitions. He gave up his mining job and travelled throughout Scotland and the north of England with touring concert parties. In 1900 Lauder went to London and was called in at the last minute to replace an act at Gatti's-in-the-Road. The audience loved him,

Lauder was sought after by agents, and played as many as four music halls in one evening. He subsequently toured America and the Commonwealth regularly. During the First World War Lauder was active in encouraging American intervention and entertained the troops on the Western Front.

Typically costumed in fantastic tartans and holding a crooked stick, Lauder interspersed his songs with comic patter. He wrote most of his own music and lyrics, drawing on traditional airs for a memorable tune. 'I love a Lassie' was sung for the first time at a Glasgow pantomime, in 1905 and 'Roamin' in the Gloamin' was performed in the New Year season of 1907.

Sir Patrick Geddes 1854–1932 by Desmond Chute

Geddes was born at Ballater in Aberdeenshire but spent his schooldays in Perth. He worked in a bank in Perth for a time and also considered becoming an artist before deciding to study biology. He subsequently worked in London under Thomas Huxley for two years. This was followed by a period studying zoology under Henri de Lacaze-Duthiers at Roscoff in Brittany and at the Sorbonne in Paris.

At the age of twenty-five, while exploring in Mexico, he suffered a brief attack of blindness, which put a conventional career as a biologist out of the question, although he remained interested in botany and evolution throughout his life. This loss became sociology's gain, as Geddes turned from the microscope to the larger study of mankind. He became interested in social reconstruction, both in the sense of the physical re-development of urban areas and the creation of community groups. His work in the Royal Mile is one of the monuments to his memory. In 1892 he acquired the Outlook Tower near Edinburgh Castle and there established the world's first sociological laboratory. In 1911 he organised the 'Cities and Town Planning' exhibition which was shown in Britain, the Continent and in India, and by the First World War, his reputation as a pioneer town planner was international. Many of his ideas – such as the need for urban structures to provide for physical and spiritual human needs, with gardens, sun-courts and neighbourly street layouts – were to become the norm of twentieth-century town planning.

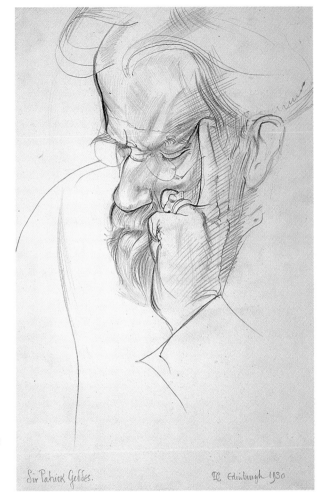

Sir Patrick Geddes.   DC. Edinburgh 1930

Pencil on paper,
33.4 × 23.7
Dated 1930
Gifted by Colin McFadyean in 1964
PG 2044

James Keir Hardie 1856–1915 by H.J. Dobson

James Keir Hardie was born into poverty near the village of Holytown in Lanarkshire and began working at the age of seven. By ten he was in the mines where he stayed for twelve years. At the same time he attended evening classes and began to agitate for better conditions and pay for miners. Blacklisted by the mine owners in 1878, he took up journalism. From that time he worked hard to establish the miners' union in Lanarkshire and in 1886 was made secretary of the Scottish miners' federation. In 1888 he stood unsuccessfully as an independent labour candidate for Parliament for North Ayrshire and in the same year the Scottish labour party was formed under his chairmanship. He started his own paper, *The Miner*, succeeded by *The Labour Leader*, which increased his influence, and in 1892 he was returned to Parliament as member for West Ham, South. He subsequently sat for Merthyr Tydfil from 1900 until his death. Keir Hardie was the first leader in the House of Commons of the Independent Labour Party and did more than any other to establish the political power of labour in Britain. He was much opposed to war and distressed by its outbreak in 1914, which undermined his health and effectively killed him the following year.

Dobson's picture shows Hardie as the successful orator, 'an excellent speaker, relying on homely phrases and simple appeals.'

Oil on canvas, 127 × 101.6
Dated 1893
Gifted by Emrys Hughes in
1952
PG 1580

James Maxton 1885–1946 by Sir John Lavery

Oil on plywood, 111.1 × 85.7
Bequeathed by the artist in 1941
PG 1416

James Maxton began his professional life as a teacher but was dismissed from his post during the First World War following imprisonment for sedition after urging the Glasgow munitions workers to strike. He then worked in the shipyards and in 1922 was chosen as the socialist candidate for Bridgeton. At Westminster he was seen as one of the wild men from the Clyde, 'determined to fight for the cause of the poor in Heaven's name or Hell's.' He rose to prominence in the Independent Labour Party and was largely responsible for building up the socialist movement in Scotland. He greatly admired the Soviet Union and advocated revolution. During the Second World War he was prominent as the leader of the 'Clydeside Trio' with John McGovern and Campbell Stephen.

The portrait by Sir John Lavery, who is better known as a painter of establishment figures, is an unexpected tribute to the charm and integrity of James Maxton – in McGovern's words 'too decent a human being for politics'.

James Ramsay Macdonald 1866–1937

James Ramsay Macdonald addressing
the House of Commons in 1924
by Sir John Lavery
Oil on panel, 39.1 × 29.2
Bought in 1994
PG 2946

Ramsay Macdonald was born in Lossiemouth, the son of a Highland ploughman, John Macdonald, and a local girl, Anne Ramsay. His parents did not marry and he lived in poverty until the 1890s when he established himself in London and married Margaret Gladstone, a middle-class socialist whose views reinforced his own rejection of Marxism. He joined the Independent Labour Party in 1894, the year after its foundation. In 1906 he was returned to Parliament, by now secretary of the Labour Party. During the troubled years before the outbreak of the First World War, Macdonald was a force for moderation, deploring industrial unrest, but urging the government to listen to the strikers' grievances. Macdonald subsequently made himself extremely unpopular through his conviction that Britain had been wrong to enter the conflict. In 1924 he formed Britain's first Labour government. This administration – in which he was both Prime Minister and Foreign Secretary – lasted only months. He was Prime Minister again from 1929 to 1935, the final four years as head of a national coalition government which his own party saw as betrayal.

This curiously introverted private portrait was exhibited at the Royal Academy in 1926, the year of the General Strike which Ramsay Macdonald had done his utmost to avert.

OPPOSITE
James Ramsay Macdonald
by Ambrose McEvoy
Oil on canvas, 99.1 × 78.7
Gifted by Sir Alexander Grant through the Scottish
Modern Arts Association in 1938
PG 1351

163

Marjory Kennedy Fraser 1857–1930 by John Duncan

As a child, Marjory Kennedy Fraser accompanied her father on his tours at home and abroad. While she played the piano, he sang Scottish folk songs. Later they performed together as the 'Singing Kennedys'. As an adult, Marjory Kennedy Fraser added Gaelic song to her repertoire, a highly popular move and one which influenced the course of her life, for it is with Gaelic music and Hebridean song in particular that her name is most closely linked.

In 1895, while lecturing on Gaelic song, she met the artist John Duncan who painted this portrait. A central figure in the Celtic revival, Duncan persuaded her to visit the Hebridean island of Eriskay where he believed some of the fast-disappearing Celtic music might still be heard. With great determination Mrs Kennedy Fraser managed to record both music and lyrics. Her first collection, *Songs of The Hebrides*, was published in 1909. It was followed by further collections. Although the authenticity of her renderings has been questioned, there is no doubt that without her, much Gaelic music of great interest and beauty would have been lost.

John Duncan, who painted this portrait in the early 1920s, has placed his friend against the landscape of Eriskay, her shawl blowing gently in the wind.

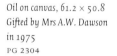

Oil on canvas, 61.2 × 50.8
Gifted by Mrs A.W. Dawson
in 1975
PG 2304

Mary Garden 1874–1967 by Mark Tobey

Chalk on paper,
63.2 × 47.4 cm
Dated 1918
Bought in 1968
PG 2133

One of the great sopranos of the twentieth century, Mary Garden (born Mary Davidson) was a native of Aberdeen. She was taken to America as a child, trained in Chicago and Paris, and began her career sensationally when she took over in the title role of Charpentier's *Louise* in mid performance at the Opéra Comique in Paris.

In 1902 she created the role of Mélisande in Debussy's *Pelléas et Mélisande* at the composer's request. She first performed in America in 1907 and was for many years involved with Chicago Grand Opera, which she directed in the early 1920s. Mary Garden returned to Scotland in 1939.

The artist Mark Tobey also trained in Chicago. He produced fashionable portrait drawings to earn a living before ultimately becoming one of America's leading abstract painters.

John Reith, Lord Reith of Stonehaven 1889–1971 by Sir Oswald Birley

John Reith's principal work began in 1922 when he was appointed as general manager of the British Broadcasting Corporation. With no precedent or example before him, he effectively created the broadcasting service at a time when even visionaries like H.G. Wells saw little future in it. He outlined the ideals of the new company in *Broadcast Over Britain* (1924) and became its first Director-General. His policy was to balance education, religion and culture alongside information and entertainment. He was adamant that the BBC should act as a force for national unity and, drawing upon his background in engineering, also insisted that the operating system should be as impressive as possible.

He left the BBC in 1938, feeling himself no longer challenged by the work, a move he later described as a 'stupendous folly'. Only his wartime service with the Royal Navy compensated for the lack of satisfaction Reith was subsequently to experience in his later appointments.

The painting is a copy of the portrait commissioned by the BBC in 1933. Reith chose the artist, who has achieved a sense of this large (six feet six inches) man's aggressive and determined nature. A large scar, received during the First World War, is just visible on his left cheek.

Oil on canvas,
127.5 × 102.3
Bought in 1981
PG 2475

John Logie Baird 1888–1946 by James Kerr-Lawson

Pencil on paper,
50.5 × 37.7
Bought in 1943
PG 1437

The son of a Church of Scotland minister, John Logie Baird was a prolific and far-sighted inventor, a pioneer of television and radar systems. He turned his mind to ideas as diverse as a patented watertight undersock and making jam from guavas in Trinidad, but is best known for transmitting the first televised images. This he did in 1923, in rented rooms in Hastings, but the achievement probably followed years of experimentation, including his time in Port of Spain, where locals, seeing strange flashing lights, suspected Baird of practising black magic. He publicly demonstrated the invention in 1926; two years later he broadcast the first pictures from London to New York, developed colour television, 'Noctovision' (transmission in darkness using infra-red) and was working on video recordings. Baird worked largely without the help of major backers. The BBC, suspicious that television was a threat to radio, gave only uneven support and, in 1937, when it was obvious that the medium could not be ignored, chose the rival electronic Marconi-EMI system. Although Baird disappeared from public view after this date, he continued to develop innovations. He died shortly after the close of the Second World War and it now seems that the 'quiet' years after the BBC's rejection of his system were spent in secret wartime work.

Eric Liddell 1902–1945 by Eileen Soper

On 10 July 1924 at the Paris Olympic Games, Eric Liddell won a gold medal in the men's 400 metres in a world-record time of 47.6 seconds. His success was all the sweeter in that he had debarred himself from competing in the 100 metres, for which he was favourite, by refusing to run in the heats because they were being held on a Sunday. Prior to this, he had won seven caps as a wing threequarter with the Scottish rugby team.

A fervent evangelical Christian, Liddell left Scotland in 1925, shortly after this portrait was painted. He took up an appointment as a missionary teacher in Tientsin near Peking. (He had been born in China, the son of Scottish missionaries.) In 1943, at the time of the Japanese invasion of China, Liddell was interned. He died in a Japanese camp two years later of a brain tumour.

In 1981 the story of his athletic career was told in the film *Chariots of Fire*.

Oil on canvas, 73.5 × 61.5
Bought in 1995
PG 2992

ERIC H. LIDDELL

John Buchan, Lord Tweedsmuir 1875–1940 by Yousuf Karsh

Silver gelatine photograph
33 × 27
Gifted by the photographer
in 1985
PGP 95.1

John Buchan, author and statesman, was born in Perth. The son of a Free Church minister, he was educated at Hutcheson's Grammar School and the universities of Glasgow and Oxford, where he won the Newdigate prize for poetry in 1898. He was called to the bar in 1901, and became private secretary to Lord Milner, the able high commissioner for South Africa. Buchan served in the First World War and at the same time wrote the part-work, *The Nelson History of the War*. He was elected to Parliament as member for the Scottish Universities and was made a peer in 1935, when he became Governor-General of Canada. In 1937, he became a privy councillor, and Chancellor of the University of Edinburgh.

John Buchan is perhaps best known for the numerous adventure stories and the spy thrillers that he wrote, which include *The Thirty-Nine Steps* (1915) and *Greenmantle* (1916). This portrait of Buchan, wearing a native Canadian headdress, was taken while he was Governor-General by the Armenian-born photographer Yousuf Karsh. Karsh wrote of Buchan: 'He was the most informal of men, impatient with the strict protocol his position sometimes demanded.'

Francis George Scott 1880–1958 by William Johnstone

Writing of his encounter with his cousin, Francis George Scott, Willie Johnstone recalled Scott's vision of 'a splendid revival, a Scottish Renaissance of the arts'. During the inter-war years composer and painter united with Hugh MacDiarmid in condemnation of the subservience of Scottish culture to English values. In his music Scott explored a distinctively Scottish idiom, drawing on the conventions of Scottish folk music and speech rhythms. His *Scottish Lyrics* (five volumes issued between 1921 and 1939) comprise his settings of songs by many of Scotland's greatest poets. But it was MacDiarmid, who had been his pupil, who perhaps inspired him most. This portrait pays tribute to the shared source of inspiration of the three great artists: poet, painter and musician in the Borders landscape.

Oil on canvas, 96.5 × 71.1
Bought in 1991
PG 2849

Sir Hugh S. Roberton 1874–1952 by William Niven

Ink on paper, 38.1 × 28.9
Gifted by Michael Donnelly
in 1966
PG 2063

Niven's witty sketch of Hugh Roberton captures those qualities of charm and savagery that a good choirmaster needs. For half a century, Roberton's name was synonymous with the Glasgow Orpheus Choir which he trained to the very highest standards. Two qualities, in particular, characterised the choir: beauty of tone and purity of enunciation. Roberton worked closely with Margery Kennedy Fraser and wrote choral arrangements of her Hebridean songs. Altogether, Roberton published about three hundred pieces of choralised Scottish folk songs, most of which are still in the repertoire. The choir, under Roberton, however, did not limit itself to Scottish music. Italian madrigals, English motets and the music of the Russian Orthodox Church all featured in its programmes.

Sir Alexander Fleming 1881–1955 by Wolfgang Suschitsky

Silver gelatine photograph,
24.4 × 27
Bought in 1983
PGP 10.1

Alexander Fleming's professional career began in 1906, when he joined the Inoculation Department of St Mary's Hospital, London, under the celebrated bacteriologist, Almroth Wright. At this time, the search was underway to find a method of destroying pathogenic bacteria without destroying the body's natural protectors, the phagocytes. During the First World War, Fleming was able to demonstrate that antiseptics could be actively harmful in treating wounds. When suffering from a cold in 1921, he discovered that nasal mucus contained a beneficial antiseptic substance he called 'lysozyme'. In 1928 he made the breakthrough discovery of the antiseptic properties of penicillium mould. This was analysed and made practical through the collaborative work of others, and the production of pure penicillin was achieved by Ernest Chain and Howard Florey in 1940. In 1942, Fleming demonstrated that penicillin could cure meningitis and the British government urged its mass production. Fleming was knighted in 1944 and shared the Nobel Prize for Medicine with Chain and Florey in 1945.

This photograph was taken when Suschitsky was making a documentary film on penicillin for the Ministry of Information in 1944.

John Boyd Orr, Lord Boyd Orr 1880–1971 *by Benno Schotz*

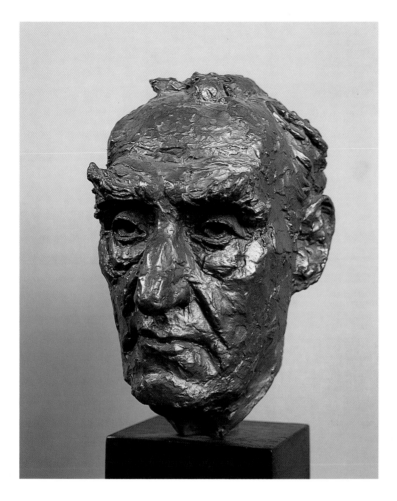

A nutritional physiologist, John Boyd Orr showed, by experiment, the value of milk in the health and growth of children. His friendship with Walter Elliot (Under-Secretary of State for Scotland from 1926 to 1929), led to legislation to provide free milk for children in all Scottish schools.

Orr continued to draw attention to the poor state of health and nutrition of the British people and advocated a national food policy linked to an agricultural policy. The political implications of this were such that the government refused to publish his findings.

After the war Orr became the first director of the United Nations Food and Agriculture Organisation. In 1949 he was awarded the Nobel Peace Prize. This bust was modelled a year later.

Bronze bust, 30 high
Bought in 1986
PG 2698

Walter Rankin (Local Defence Volunteer) by Sir William Oliphant Hutchison

When this portrait was bought by the Scottish National Portrait Gallery, the identity of the sitter had been lost. The importance of the portrait for the Gallery lay chiefly in the type represented: a member of a Local Defence Volunteer unit – a nation-wide body of men, known popularly as the Home Guard, too old for military service overseas, who nevertheless wanted to play their part in the defence of Great Britain against German aggression.

After the portrait had been acquired, the identity of the soldier was rediscovered. He was Walter Rankin, a retired newsagent and a member of the Skelmorlie LDV, later the Skelmorlie Home Guard.

W.O. Hutchison, at the time the Director of Glasgow School of Art, was in Rankin's home guard unit. He chose to paint the soldier as a symbol of national resilience and resistance. When the portrait was first exhibited, it was with these lines from Shakespeare's King John: 'Come the three corners of the world in arms, and we shall shock them.'

Oil on canvas, 76 × 55.6
Dated 1940
Bought in 1987
PG 2719

'Existence Precarious' by Robert Henderson Blyth

The artist, Robert Henderson Blyth
(1919–70), joined the Royal Army
Medical Corps in 1941 and served
widely in Europe throughout the
Second World War. During his
service he carried a lamp in his pack
which, when fitted with a yellow
bulb, gave an approximation of
daylight, allowing him to paint
during the hours of darkness.

This picture was painted at the
end of hostilities and shows a
soldier, who appears to be the artist
himself, exhausted by the conflict, a
colleague, possibly dead, beside
him, and the world in ruins behind.
This is not a celebration of victory
but a stark view of a world devastated
by war.

Oil on panel, 65.4 × 80.3
Bought in 1991
PG 2851

Sir Basil Spence 1907–1976 by Lida Moser

Born in India of Scots parents, Basil Spence studied architecture in Edinburgh and London. After qualifying in 1933, Spence worked in the London office of Sir Edwin Lutyens, assisting him with drawings for the vice-regal buildings in New Delhi; he then returned to Edinburgh to set up in practice. After the Second World War, Spence became known as a leading exhibition designer, most notably for his pavilion in the 1951 Festival of Britain exhibition. In the same year he won the competition to design a new cathedral for Coventry. This building became an emblem of national regeneration and reconstruction and brought Spence admiration and fame. The preservation of the shell of the old cathedral, together with Spence's inclusion of specially commissioned works of art by Graham Sutherland, John Piper and Jacob Epstein, underlined its symbolic role. Now acclaimed as Britain's most prominent architect, he went on to design many of the new universities, including Sussex, and to provide modern facilities for old institutions (undergraduate residences at Queen's College, Cambridge; Edinburgh University Library). Spence also worked on more modest schemes, such as fishermen's cottages at Dunbar and Newhaven.

Lida Moser's photograph was one of a number taken by her for American *Vogue* in 1947.

Eric Linklater 1899–1974 by Lida Moser

Like Byron before him, Eric Linklater was educated at Aberdeen Grammar School and the humorous, picaresque novel by which he is perhaps best known, *Juan in America* (1931), tells the adventures of Juan Motley, a descendant of Byron's Don Juan, let loose on the United States during the prohibition years. 'As originally conceived', wrote Linklater, very possibly tongue in cheek, 'it was to have been written in verse – Byronic stanzas – but having begun to take pleasure in the looser and more variable rhythms of prose, and flinching when it came to the point of finding thirty thousand rhymes, I unhorsed the infant poem in its first canto and bade it walk'.

Juan in America was the product of two years as a Commonwealth fellow in the United States. Many of Linklater's other novels draw on his varied experiences: as a Scottish National Party candidate at the East Fife by-election in 1933 (*Magnus Merriman*), service in Italy during the Second World War (*Private Angelo*) and Edinburgh during the 1950s (*The Merry Muse*). But it is with Orkney, the land of his ancestors and for many years his own home, that Linklater's name is most closely attached and whose distinctive identity inspired so much of his writing.

Silver gelatine photograph,
30.4 × 25.4
Bought in 1984
PGP 43.5

Douglas Douglas-Hamilton, 14th Duke of Hamilton 1903–1973 and Elizabeth, Duchess of Hamilton b.1916 *by Oskar Kokoschka*

Oil on canvas,
89.8 × 129.8
Bought with help from the
National Art Collections
Fund, the National Heritage
Memorial Fund and the
Pilgrim Trust in 1987
PG 2723

The Duke of Hamilton's gentle manner was belied by an active life of great variety. In his youth he was known as 'the boxing Marquis' and won the Scottish amateur middle-weight title. Also a pioneer aviator, he was the chief pilot of the first flight over Mount Everest in 1933, and during the Second World War he commanded the Air Training Corps in Scotland. One bizarre wartime episode brought unsought for notoriety: in 1941 Rudolph Hess flew, uninvited, from Nazi Germany to the Douglas-Hamilton's Lanarkshire estates in the misguided belief that he could somehow open lines of communication with the British establishment. Post war, the Duke maintained his interest in aviation and held various important positions in the royal household. The duchess, as well as supporting her husband's public life, has played an active part in the cultural activities of the Lothians.

This painting was commissioned by the duke. His son had noticed Kokoschka's work at the Tate Gallery in 1962 and, impressed by the expressiveness of the portraits, recommended him to his father. When the sitters first met, Kokoschka warned them, 'You do not want to be painted by me, my art is cruel!', but they were not deterred. Kokoschka spent a month at Lennoxlove where the artist quickly 'got' the duke; the figure of the duchess was repainted several times. The resultant image, vividly textural and vibrantly colourful, suggests both the characters of the sitters and their relationship.

Queen Elizabeth, the Queen Mother b.1900 by *Avigdor Arikha*

Born Elizabeth Bowes-Lyon, the youngest daughter of the 14th Earl of Strathmore, the Queen Mother is descended from King Robert II of Scotland. She was born in England but during her childhood part of every year was spent at Glamis Castle in Angus. In 1923 she married the Duke of York, who became King George VI unexpectedly after his brother's abdication in 1936. This was a period of crisis for the monarchy, and, as Queen Elizabeth at the side of her rather shy husband, the Queen Mother was instrumental in restoring respect for the institution. The decision of the king and queen to remain in London during the blitz and not to send the two princesses, Elizabeth and Margaret, to Canada, was an important symbolic act. The Queen Mother has always enjoyed the affection of the British public and has been described as having an astonishing gift of manifesting genuine interest.

This portrait was the first commissioned by the Scottish National Portrait Gallery to record eminent living Scots. Appropriately, the Queen Mother is known for her own interest in collecting twentieth-century art, an enthusiasm which sets her apart from other family members but one which co-exists with her other, more traditional loves of fishing, horse-racing and gardening.

Oil on canvas, 49.7 × 50.3
Commissioned by the Gallery in 1983
PG 2598

Hugh MacDiarmid (pen name of Christopher Murray Grieve) 1892–1978

Poets' Pub
by Alexander Moffat
Oil on canvas, 183 × 244
Dated 1980
Bought in 1983
PG 2597

OPPOSITE
Hugh MacDiarmid
by Robert Heriot Westwater
Oil on canvas,
112.3 × 86.7 · Dated 1962
Acquired from the sitter's
estate in 1978
PG 2604

Although much of MacDiarmid's writing is in English, for example the long poem, *In Memoriam James Joyce* (1955), his greatest contribution to the Scottish literary renaissance was his creation of a dynamic and lyrical Scots language, both intellectual and colloquial, with which to replace the sentimentality of so much Scottish poetry, especially of the nineteenth century. Always passionately concerned with Scottish identity (the subject of his early masterpiece, *A Drunk Man looks at the Thistle*), he was a founder member of the Scottish National Party, but his instincts were equally international and influenced by Marxism. MacDiarmid was probably the major cultural influence in Scotland this century, at the heart of a movement which had an impact far beyond merely literary circles.

Westwater's portrait, subtitled 'Lucky Poet' (after his autobiography of the same name, published in 1943), was commissioned by public subscription to celebrate MacDiarmid's seventieth birthday, and presented to him in Henry Raeburn's former studio at 32 York Place, a few steps from the Scottish National Portrait Gallery.

In Alexander Moffat's group portrait *Poets' Pub*, MacDiarmid is shown amid the major Scottish poets and writers of the second half of the twentieth century, set in an amalgam of their favourite Edinburgh drinking haunts – Milne's Bar, the Abbotsford and the Café Royal. From left to right, they are: Norman MacCaig, Hugh MacDiarmid, Sorley Maclean, Ian Crichton Smith, George Mackay Brown, Sydney Goodsir Smith, Edwin Morgan and Robert Garioch. In the foreground is Alan Bold and, on the steps behind, the art critic John Tonge.

Dr Winifred Rushforth 1885–1983 by Victoria Crowe

Oil on hardboard,
56 × 76.3
Bought in 1982
PG 2519

'They shall know we are old, not by the frailty of the body but by the strength and creativity of the psyche.' Victoria Crowe chose this saying of Dr Rushforth to characterise her portrait of the most remarkable pioneer of group psychoanalytical therapy in Scotland. Dr Rushforth became particularly interested in dreams and their interpretation as described by Freud and Jung, and it was through one of her dream groups in Edinburgh that the artist met her future sitter.

Dr Rushforth is shown beside a sculpture of a Bushman. She appears to be listening to his 'song from the soul' as described in Laurens van der Post's short story *Mantis Carol*. But the image of a wise old woman listening is one that remained in the minds of many of the people who attended Dr Rushforth's dream groups and other psychoanalytical sessions.

Alexander Sutherland Neill 1883–1973 by Ishbel McWhirter

A.S. Neill developed his radical ideas on child education partly as a reaction to his own dismal experience as a school-boy, and then as a teacher, within the rigid and highly disciplined confines of the Victorian school system. Neill followed the profession of his parents, school-teachers in Angus, but moving to London, and then abroad, in the 1920s, brought him into a sympathetic and progressive milieu. Here, influenced by Freud and the work of the New Educational Fellowship, he evolved an alternative definition of education in tune with his optimistic view of human nature, where emotions were more important than intellect and children would develop free from fear.

Summerhill, founded in 1924, is the school synonymous with A.S. Neill. The essential quality of Summerhill was, according to Neill, freedom and self-government, "self-government for the pupils and staff, freedom to go to lessons or stay away, freedom to play for days or weeks or years if necessary...". Summerhill confounded expectations that this would lead to anarchy and empty class-rooms and it was seen as evidence of the experiment's success that creativity was encouraged rather than the pursuit of conventional academic goals. Ishbel McWhirter was herself a pupil at Summerhill.

Oil on canvas, 76.2 × 61
Bought in 1985
PG 2638

Sir Steven Runciman b.1903 by Stephen Conroy

Sir Steven Runciman is an outstanding historian of Byzantine civilisation and his three volume *History of the Crusades*, published in the early 1950s, has become a classic of narrative historical writing. He was educated at Eton and Trinity College, Cambridge where he was a fellow and later honorary fellow. For many years Sir Steven was president of the British Institute of Archaeology at Ankara and served as chairman of the Anglo-Hellenic League. It was Sir Steven's choice to commission Stephen Conroy to paint his portrait, destined from the start for the Scottish National Portrait Gallery. Conroy was sixty years younger than his sitter but had already enjoyed phenomenal success. Four years before this portrait was painted, Conroy held his degree show at Glasgow School of Art which launched his career.

The artist spent a weekend with Sir Steven at the historian's Dumfriesshire home. The portrait, which captures the sitter's urbanity and intelligence, was subsequently painted in the artist's studio.

Oil on canvas, 122 × 76.2
Commissioned by friends of the sitter and presented to the Gallery in 1990
PG 2818

Sir Ludovic Kennedy b.1919 and Moira Shearer b.1926 *by Avigdor Arikha*

Ludovic Kennedy and Moira Shearer married in 1950. Shearer shot to fame in 1948 with her role as the doomed young ballerina in Michael Powell and Emeric Pressburger's film, *The Red Shoes*. Born in Dunfermline, she made her debut on the stage at the Alhambra Theatre in Glasgow in 1941 as a soloist with Mona Inglesby's International Ballet Company and joined Sadler's Wells the following year. During the next decade Shearer danced all the major classical roles and created that of Cinderella. From 1952 she combined family life (she and Kennedy have four children) with a second career as an actress and lecturer.

A pioneer of television broadcasting, Edinburgh-born Kennedy became a newscaster in 1956 and presented some of the first current affairs programmes, most notably, *Panorama*, broadcast by the BBC. In the 1960s Kennedy turned his investigative and journalistic expertise to miscarriages of justice; his book, *10 Rillington Place*, eventually led to a posthumous pardon for Timothy Evans, executed for the murders committed by John Christie. Since then, whilst working at the top of his profession in broadcasting, Kennedy has exposed some of the most notorious cases of injustice in Britain.

Oil on canvas, 79.5 × 99.5
Commissioned by the Gallery in 1993
PG 2923

Alexander Douglas-Home, Lord Home of the Hirsel 1903–1995
by Avigdor Arikha

Lord Home, better known as Alec Douglas-Home, was one of the most important Conservative statesmen of this century, whose long political career spanned a period of over fifty years. From a privileged background (the Douglas-Home family owned great estates in the Lowlands), the young Lord Dunglass entered Parliament as a Unionist in 1931 after winning the marginal seat of Lanark. He became Parliamentary Private Secretary to Neville Chamberlain, whom he accompanied to Germany in 1938 on the government's abortive attempt to appease Hitler and Mussolini.

After the war, Lord Home emerged as a key figure in world affairs. He was appointed Commonwealth Secretary in 1955 and Foreign Secretary in 1960. In 1963, after Harold Macmillan's resignation, he briefly became Prime Minister, disclaiming his peerage and fighting a by-election in order to sit in the House of Commons. The Conservatives lost the election the following year but in 1970 Home returned to the post of Foreign Secretary under Edward Heath, which he held until 1974 when he was made a life peer. Described as the 'quiet aristocrat of British politics', Lord Home was widely respected as a man of integrity with a strong sense of public duty.

Oil on canvas, 91.5 × 71.3
Commissioned by the
Gallery in 1988
PG 2736

Jo (Joseph) Grimond, Lord Grimond 1913–1993 *by Patrick Heron*

Oil on canvas, 121 × 91.5
Commissioned by the
Gallery in 1987
PG 2717

'Jo' Grimond was leader of the Parliamentary Liberal Party from 1956 to 1967 and represented Orkney and Shetland in the House of Commons for thirty-three years. He was born in St Andrews, from where his father, a wealthy jute manufacturer, commuted daily to Dundee. After Eton and Oxford, he decided to become a Liberal politician and his marriage to Asquith's granddaughter confirmed his membership of an old governing élite. His mother-in-law, Lady Bonham-Carter, once declared, 'he is destined for No.10', but, after the Second World War, such a destiny was unlikely with the Liberal Party on the verge of extinction. Grimond's reversal of this seemingly inevitable process was one of his greatest political achievements. His aim was to make his party the radical alternative to Conservatism, and through the force of his personality and vision, the Liberals doubled their representation at Westminster and tripled their share of the vote during his leadership.

Grimond had visited neither Orkney nor Shetland before 1945, but he made the Old Manse, Kirkwall, his home and when he was made a life peer in 1983, took the title Baron Grimond of Firth in the County of Orkney. After relinquishing the leadership of the Liberal Party he became particularly concerned with Scottish issues and was an early advocate of devolution of power from Westminster.

Ronald David Laing 1927–1989 by Victoria Crowe

Oil on hardboard,
91.4 × 71.1
Dated 1984
Commissioned by the
Gallery in 1984
PG 2616

This portrait was unveiled at the Scottish National Portrait Gallery on the occasion of the publication of the first volume of R.D. Laing's autobiography, *Wisdom, Madness and Folly*. In it, the radical psychiatrist described his life up to the year 1960, when he published his first and most famous work, *The Divided Self*, and left his native Glasgow for London.

The Divided Self became a cult book in the '60s, that cultish decade. It was a study of sanity and madness and its basic purpose was to make madness, and the process of going mad, comprehensible. Laing's opinion on the relative sanity of psychiatrists and their patients outraged many in the profession. Controversial too, was his view that, in confining people in mental hospitals, psychiatrists were functioning as agents of a repressive society.

Ian Hamilton Finlay b.1925 by Robin Gillanders

The artist, poet and writer Ian Hamilton Finlay was born in the Bahamas of Scottish parents. He was brought up in Scotland and trained at Glasgow School of Art. In the 1950s he began to write, playing an important role in the foundation of the 'concrete poetry' movement of the 1960s. Subsequently, the major concern of his art has been the relationship between words and images.

Since 1966, Finlay has lived at Dunsyre in the Pentland Hills near Edinburgh. He has made a garden, Little Sparta, that has become one of his most important artistic expressions. In it, sculpture and carved inscriptions, often making classical allusions or reflecting his fascination with the French Revolution, are 'discovered' in the landscape. Robin Gillanders has worked with Ian Hamilton Finlay on several projects and has photographed Little Sparta extensively. Of his portrait of Finlay, Gillanders has said: 'Ian, amongst other things is interested in boats and the sea, and a lot of his work deals with that, it is one of his persisting themes. Each of the photographs is mounted onto canvas, which has little tears and rents in it. This echoes slightly the idea of a sail'. Finlay is shown in a rowing boat on one of the ponds in his garden.

Composite photographic work,
120 × 90
Bought in 1995
PGP 184.20

Bill Gibb 1943–1988 by Michael Leonard

Born the son of a farmer at New Pitsligo in Aberdeenshire, Bill Gibb revolutionised British fashion during the 1970s and '80s. He counted Twiggy, Bianca Jagger and Elizabeth Taylor amongst his customers.

He was particularly famous for his evening wear, with fantastic, floating chiffon dresses and supple jersey dresses adorned with appliqué and embroidery. He was also one of the first designers to introduce ethnic clothes and he pioneered the combina-tion of several different patterned fabrics in one costume.

Michael Leonard's *trompe l'oeil* drawing simulates a plate from an illustrated book, with Bill Gibb as a sixteenth-century knight. Perhaps the artist intended to comment on the sitter's own ability, through fashion, to change the appearance of his clients.

Pencil on paper,
31.6 × 26.8
Bought in 1994
PG 2945

Detail from Plate 139

Jean Muir 1928–1995 by Glenys Barton

Jean Muir began her working life in the shops of Liberty and Jaeger in London and effectively taught herself design. She launched her 'Jane and Jane' label through Susan Small and set up her own independent business in 1966. Even at that date, her work had achieved its characteristic style, described as a 'calm in a psychedelic storm'. For thirty years she specialised in the skills of cutting and draping material to achieve a deceptive sense of simplicity. She preferred to think of herself as a dressmaker rather than a designer and referred to 'engineering' with fabric. Her clothes were sensual and carefully structured, based on intricate patterns of up to fifty pieces, designed to move with the body. She was a favourite designer with her famous customers and the fashion editors.

Glenys Barton's portrait catches Jean Muir's attachment to her Scottish ancestry, which she felt gave her the ability to be objectively ruthless without any fear of unnecessary sentiment.

Ceramic with glazed slip,
44 high
Bought in 1993
PG 2939

Dame Muriel Spark b.1919 by Alexander Moffat

As a child at school in Edinburgh, Muriel Spark and her classmates fell under the spell of a remarkable teacher, Christina Kay. Miss Kay's girls were special. They were an élite, educated out of hours by expeditions round their historic city and by visits to the theatre and ballet where they discovered a sense of their own importance as citizens of Edinburgh and the world. As Muriel Spark later wrote, Miss Kay was a character in search of an author and in the eleven year-old school girl she found that author. Miss Kay became Miss Brodie, the heroine of Muriel Spark's most famous novel, *The Prime of Miss Jean Brodie*.

Good and evil are the warp and weft of Muriel Spark's many novels, something she shares with the greatest Scottish writers like James Hogg and Robert Louis Stevenson. 'I am a poet but I'm attracted to clarity, to clear, sparse detail.' Muriel Spark was writing about her own prose style, but she might equally have been describing the art of Alexander Moffat, now Head of Painting at Glasgow School of Art, who was commissioned to paint this portrait in 1984.

Oil on canvas, 183 × 91.4
Commissioned by the Gallery in 1984
PG 2617

Alasdair Gray b.1934 by Iain Stewart

Alasdair Gray is one of the most successful and original of contemporary Scotish writers. He was born in Glasgow where he studied drawing and painting at the School of Art. His first novel, *Lanark*, was published in 1981. It achieved great critical acclaim and its experimental and innovatory treatment of language prompted comparisons with James Joyce. Subsequent works include *Something Leather*, *McGrotty and Ludmilla*, *A History Maker*, and *Poor Things*. Gray is an advocate of a Scottish Parliament, and his political writings include *Why Scots Should Rule Scotland*.

This photograph by Iain Stewart is one of a series in which people were asked to make a self-portrait and pose with it before the camera. The device of deflecting or displacing the self-consciousness of the sitter produced interesting results. Here, Gray's own rather well-rehearsed caricature is offered for comparison with the 'real thing'.

Silver gelatine photograph,
25 × 25
Bought in 1994
PGP 153.5

George Mackay Brown 1921–1996 by Pradip Malde

The poet, novelist and short story writer, George Mackay Brown, was born in Stromness on the mainland of Orkney. His mother was a crofter-fisherman's daughter and his father was the local tailor and postman. Due to the onset of tuberculosis in his teens, Brown was unable to attend university, do military service or go to sea. It was not until he was in his late thirties that he attended the University of Edinburgh, after a formative period at Newbattle Abbey College under the poet Edwin Muir. In these years he became a member of the circle of distinguished poets in the capital, which included Sydney Goodsir Smith and Norman MacCaig.

After this sojourn in Edinburgh, Brown returned to Orkney where he spent the rest of his life. His writings draw on Orcadian folklore, tales of the sea and Scandinavian sagas. A convert to Roman Catholicism at the age of forty, his work is marked by a spirituality and a kind of Christian fatalism. Another poet, Douglas Dunn, has said of him: 'He was very unusual among Scottish poets in that there is not a trace of aggression in his work'. In some ways he might be seen as the poetic antithesis of Hugh MacDiarmid. Brown's character was gentle, benevolent and melancholic. In a revealing passage of his autobiography he writes: 'The first line of Shakespeare that I experienced intrigued me: "I sooth, I know not why I am so sad / It wearies me...". These words should be carved over the lintel of my door: in a way they express perfectly my life and my way of looking at things – a tremulous melancholy, a mystery through which are glimpsed and guessed from time to time forms beauty and delight'.

Platinum photograph,
23.9 × 18.4
Bought in 1987
PGP 100.9

Sir Peter Maxwell Davies b.1934 by John Bellany

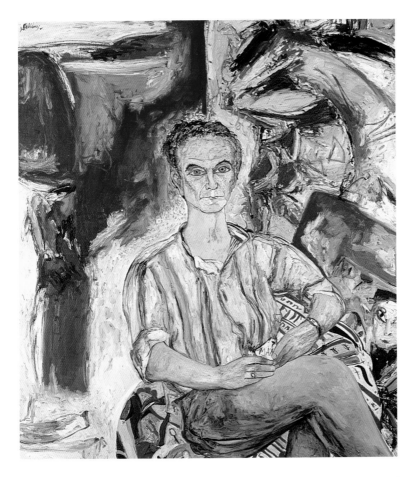

Oil on canvas,
172.5 × 152.4
Commissioned by the
Gallery in 1991
PG 2888

'I was immediately struck by the man's piercing black eyes (like Picasso's), as soon as I opened the door', wrote the painter, John Bellany, about Peter Maxwell Davies, the composer whom he had been commissioned to paint.

'He had a charisma – here was a man who was somebody – a creative artist of the top tier. I knew before the brush touched the canvas I could do something extraordinary.'

Maxwell Davies and Bellany spoke about the Island of Hoy where the composer lives and which has been the inspiration for much of his work, of George Mackay Brown, the Orkney writer and a mutual friend, and of Orkney's St Magnus Festival which Maxwell Davies directed. At the start of his career Sir Peter studied at the Royal Manchester College of Music in the city where he was born. Early English music has been a lifelong interest, indeed the sixteenth-century composer, John Taverner, is the subject of one of his operas.

Artist and composer discussed the creative act itself and found much common ground: 'The painting blossomed, a friendship was born and the whole experience was a joy.'

Sean Connery b.1930 by Annie Leibovitz

Silver gelatine photograph,
35.2 × 42.5
Gifted by the photographer
in 1994
PGP 158.1

Sean Connery was born in Edinburgh and began his working life in jobs as various as milkman, lifeguard, coffin-polisher and artists' model. He made his theatrical debut in the chorus line of the London production of *South Pacific* in 1951. He then moved into film and television work. His great public success began with the James Bond movies, starting with *Dr No* in 1962, which made him a top box-office draw and international film star. His career has, however, successfully avoided type-casting and the impressive range of characters he has portrayed in films like *The Hill* of 1965, *The Molly Maguires* in 1968 and *The Man Who Would be King* in 1975, has been recognised in the BAFTA award for his 1987 film, *The Name of the Rose*, and an Oscar in 1988 for his part in *The Untouchables*. Connery has said that although many of his films were action pictures, he prefers the quiet, human moments on screen.

Sean Connery's interest in politics has led him to lend his support to the Scottish National Party and the idea of the new Scottish Parliament. He has also endowed the Scottish Education Trust with the profits of the film *Diamonds Are Forever*.

Annie Leibovitz's photograph of Sean Connery, taken in the Bahamas in 1993, is an image of contained strength and intelligence.

Rikki Fulton b.1924 by Thomas Kluge

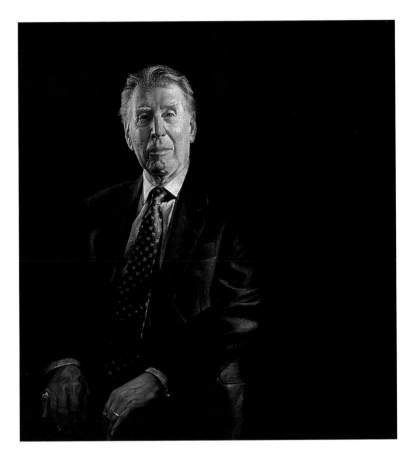

Regarded as one of the finest comic actors of his generation, Rikki Fulton's career has spanned theatre and pantomime, radio, television and film. Apart from a period in London hosting BBC Radio's *Show Band Show*, Fulton has chosen primarily to work in Scotland and lives in Glasgow, where he was born. His humour, with its roots in traditional variety acts, has a particularly Scottish appeal, with characters such as the Revd I. M. Jolly, the melancholic Church of Scotland minister, who regularly saw in Hogmany on television's *Scotch and Wry* show.

One of his best loved creations is a double act of a pair of Glasgow teddy boys called Francie and Josie, a routine which first appeared at the Alhambra Theatre, Glasgow in 1959. Jack Milroy plays Francie to Fulton's Josie and the sketches (written by Fulton) are renowned for spinning off into surreal ad-libs. Fulton has described making a live audience laugh helplessly as 'an indescribable joy ... it is what everyone craves to be able to do'.

Acrylic on canvas, 80.5 × 80.5
Commissioned by the Gallery in 1997
PG 3033

David Steel, Lord Steel of Aikwood b.1938 *by John Bratby*

Born in Fife, the son of a minister of the Church of Scotland, David Steel was educated in Edinburgh and Nairobi. He was president of the Liberal club at university and became the youngest member of the House of Commons in 1965 when he won the Roxburgh, Selkirk and Peebles by-election. From 1983 to 1997 he represented the Borders constituency of Tweeddale, Ettrick and Lauderdale. The most notable event of Steel's early career was his sponsorship of a private member's bill to liberalise the law on abortion; he was also active in the anti-apartheid movement. In 1976 he became leader of the Liberal Party. He went on to negotiate an electoral pact with the Labour Party and an alliance with the Social Democratic Party, with whom the Liberals merged in 1988. He was knighted in 1990 and created a life peer in 1997. Although now something of an elder statesman, Steel cannot be said to have eschewed controversial causes as his recent championing of the countryside movement demonstrates.

Oil on canvas, 45 × 45
On loan from the sitter
PGL 356

John Smith 1938–1994 *by Adam Elder*

Born in Ardrishaig in the West Highlands, John Smith was the son of the village schoolmaster. He was educated at Dunoon Grammar School and the University of Glasgow where he read law. He was called to the Scottish bar in 1967, becoming a Queen's Council in 1983. In 1970 he became Labour MP for Lanarkshire North, and from 1983 for Monklands East. Smith served in the Labour administrations of Harold Wilson and James Callaghan, becoming Secretary of State for Trade in 1979. During the Thatcher administration he sat on the opposition front bench, eventually as shadow chancellor and shadow home secretary under the leadership of Neil Kinnock.

Smith achieved great success as a formidable parliamentarian. His support for Scottish devolution was a significant contribution to the Labour Party's subsequent commitment to this policy. In 1988 he suffered a heart attack and considered leaving political life. However, as a key figure in the Labour Party's recovery after their disappointment in the 1987 general election, he determined to return to Westminster. The symbol of his recovery was the very public challenge he set himself of climbing the Scottish Munros (any mountain over 3,000 feet).

Smith attained the leadership of the Labour Party in 1992 but was to suffer a second, fatal heart attack in May 1994. His death was greeted with dismay across the party divide. Many tributes were paid to John Smith as a politician of great integrity whose political ideology was founded on his sincerely held Christian beliefs.

Silver gelatine photograph, 21 × 30
Bought in 1994
PGP 157.1

Michael (Mick) McGahey b.1925 by Maggi Hambling

Mick McGahey was born in Shotts, the son of a miner. He became a miner himself at the age of fourteen. He was soon involved in union affairs and by 1949 was chairman of the Scottish Miners' Youth Committee. Increasingly in the public eye and soon to be a household name, McGahey went on to become a member of the executive of the Scottish Area of his union, vice-president in 1961 and president in 1967. In 1973 he became national vice-president, a position he held for fourteen years.

Distinctive in voice and looks, his working life was never far from controversy, often of ardent dispute. But no one could doubt Mick McGahey's dedication to the welfare of the mining communities from which he had sprung.

Oil on canvas, 122 × 96.5
Commissioned by the
Gallery in 1988
PG 2747

Sir Adam Thomson b.1926 by John Wonnacott

A former Fleet Air Arm pilot and flying instructor, Adam Thomson founded Caledonian Airways in 1961. He built up the company, later British Caledonian Airways, to become the main private enterprise rival to the state-owned British Airways. Sir Adam, knighted in 1983, was the company's chairman and chief executive. Ironically, a government committed to the free market allowed British Airways to swallow the independent airline in 1987.

This portrait was painted in Hanger 3 of Gatwick Airport, the focus of British Caledonian's operations. It is a portrait of a business as much as of its chairman and encapsulates a great enterprise.

Oil on board, 243.9 × 243.9
Dated 1986
Commissioned by the Gallery in 1986
PG 2697

Jean Redpath b.1937 by Alexander Fraser

Born in Edinburgh and raised in the kingdom of Fife, the singer Jean Redpath studied at the University of Edinburgh. Through the School of Scottish Studies she became aware of the rich tradition of Scottish folk music and became deeply involved in it. She is now internationally known as a singer of traditional Scots ballads and is the world's pre-eminent interpreter of the songs of Robert Burns. For twenty years Jean Redpath worked with the American composer Serge Hovey to produce the most extensive collection of Burns's songs ever published.

This portrait, by Alexander Fraser, was painted to celebrate Jean Redpath's sixtieth birthday. The artist has shown the singer dressed as she often performs and with a glimpse of the East Neuk of Fife on the right. The portrait, which was destined from the start for the Scottish National Portrait Gallery, is a tribute from Jean Redpath's native Fife.

Oil on canvas,
116.8 × 110.6
Commissioned by
Glenrothes and District
Burns Club and presented to
the Gallery in 1998
PG 3110

Jimmy Shand b.1908 *by George Bruce*

Oil on canvas, 90.5 × 70.8
Commissioned by a trust
established by the Earl of
Elgin and presented to the
Gallery in 1996
PG 3009

Jimmy Shand is one of the most famous names in popular Scottish music. In the late 1940s and '50s, with his chosen instrument, the accordion, he created the archetypical Scottish country dance band out of the international twentieth-century dance band sound.

He was born at East Wemyss in Fife. At the age of fourteen he became a miner at the local pit where he stayed until the general strike of 1926. After a period of occasional work by day and performing in the evenings, Jimmy Shand found more reliable employment as a demonstrator for a firm selling musical instruments.

Jimmy Shand established his own band, which gradually achieved national and, later, international acclaim. In this he was helped by radio broadcasts and, after the Second World War, television. Jimmy Shand and his band regularly ushered in the New Year to millions of listeners.

Aly Bain b.1945 by David Williams

Cibachrome photograph,
30.5 × 25.2
Gifted by the photographer
in 1994
PGP 117.31

This famous fiddler, a violin player in a traditional Scottish style, was born in Lerwick in Shetland. He has achieved fame with his group, 'the Boys of the Lough'. Bain also plays solo. David Williams recounts how the portrait came about: 'I put down a bottle of whisky and an ashtray and he played for four or five hours non-stop. He knew it was all going to be out of focus. I told him it would be nothing he could use for book covers or anything, but he used it for his record sleeve, which I was very happy with... It was a great experience. To have an exchange with someone like that is just a great privilege.'

Michael Clark b.1962 by David Williams

Silver gelatine photograph,
35.5 × 35.5
Commissioned by the
Gallery in 1988
PGP 117.5

The dancer and choreographer Michael Clark was born in Aberdeen. He was accepted by the Royal Ballet School at the age of thirteen, and went on to dance with the Royal Ballet and Ballet Rambert. He started his own company in 1984. His original and often controversial style has been described as 'incorporating punk, 1960s fantasy, nudity, video, platform shoes and giant hamburgers'. Clark has been notorious for what is, in the context of his profession, an unconventional life style involving drugs and alcohol.

Of this commission, David Williams has said: 'Michael Clark is a dangerous lunatic in the nicest possible way. He's a very strange man. When I tracked him down he was lying on a baked bean encrusted carpet under a union jack with a huge video screen and he would just watch films of himself all day. We went for breakfast, this was four o'clock in the afternoon, and he had chicken livers and bottles of wine ... I composed the thing in my head and then casually asked if I could take his portrait, shaking inside because I knew it was this or nothing. I think I got it actually. This lovely knee, bursting through the jeans – it's almost violent – and a nice juxtaposition with the gorgeous smooth head ... I'm quite happy with it'.

Sir Alexander Gibson 1926–1995 by John Houston

The Scottish National Orchestra was founded at the end of the nineteenth century but until the early 1950s was only part time. Alexander Gibson, who was born in Motherwell and trained in Glasgow, London and Europe, was appointed artistic director and principal conductor in 1959. He was the first native-born Scot to hold the posts. Gibson stayed with the orchestra for twenty-five years, raising it to a new level of excellence and using it as a means of introducing many new works to Scotland, often before they had been heard in London.

With the composer Robin Orr, Gibson played a leading role in the creation of Scottish Opera in 1962. As its artistic director he was responsible for, among many other things, the first complete performance of Berlioz's *Les Troyens* and the first production in Scotland of Wagner's *Ring* cycle in German.

Oil on canvas, 127 × 101.6
Dated 1985
Gifted by the artist in 1986
PG 2691

James MacMillan b.1959 by *Calum Colvin*

When the Scottish National Portrait Gallery decided to commission a portrait of the composer, James MacMillan, the artist, Calum Colvin, was chosen for a number of specific reasons. He is an exact contemporary of MacMillan and, like him, has already enjoyed considerable success. But, most importantly, Calum Colvin's methods of constructing his works of art invited comparison with musical composition.

Calum Colvin initially trained as a sculptor. To make his photographic works, he constructs a set in his studio, using furniture and ornaments, and then paints images on to these three-dimensional objects. When seen through the lens of his camera, a two-dimensional image is formed, a blend of reality and illusion.

Colvin visited MacMillan in his Glasgow home to see where and how he worked. Colvin then constructed a set in his Edinburgh studio. The Gallery had asked the artist to make reference to a work James MacMillan was composing at the time, his first full-length opera, *Ines de Castro*. Scottish Opera, which had commissioned the piece and first performed it at the 1996 Edinburgh International Festival, lent the model for the stage set. This was included in the portrait as were the manuscripts of the opening and closing bars of the piece. Calum Colvin also made reference to MacMillan's personal interests, including his Roman Catholic faith and his passionate support of Glasgow Celtic Football Club.

Cibachrome photograph, 154 × 123
Commissioned by the Gallery in 1996
PGP 83.14

Daniel Fergus McGrain b.1950 by Humphrey Ocean

Danny McGrain is one of the near-legendary figures in the history of Scottish football. He joined Glasgow Celtic in 1967, the year in which they became the first ever British team to win the European Cup. This was a prelude to more than a decade of unparalleled success for Celtic, to which McGrain made a vital contribu- tion. A man of unswerving loyalty and dedication, he stayed with Celtic for twenty years and won a record sixty-two caps for Scotland. At the height of his achievement he was probably the finest full-back in the world. He was twice seriously injured and struggled with the effects of diabetes throughout the greater part of his playing life.

Oil on canvas,
198.5 × 122.5
Commissioned by the
Gallery in 1989
PG 2782

208

Ralph Glasser b.1920 by Humphrey Ocean

Ralph Glasser is best-known for his trilogy of books tracing his life from Glasgow in the 1930s to Oxford University and post-war London. The first in the series, *Growing up in the Gorbals*, was published in 1986, and was followed at two-yearly intervals by *Gorbals Boy at Oxford* and *Gorbals Voices, Siren Songs*. Glasser's account of his childhood and adolescence describes the now vanished world of the Jewish immigrants in the slums of Glasgow, oppressed by the poverty and anti-semitism of the twenties and thirties. Glasser, who left school at 14 to work as a barber's soap boy and a presser in a garment factory, educated himself in the evenings and won a scholarship to Oxford University. He entered this new, and alien, world (where 'someone from the Gorbals *was* in effect a bushman, and the Gorbals itself as distant, as unknowable, as the Kalahari Desert') by cycling from Glasgow with his belongings in his saddlebag. The transition was painful, Glasser's guilt at 'escaping' from his background compounded by a growing awareness of events in Europe.

Ralph Glasser, as an economist and psychologist, later concerned himself with international development issues. Particularly concerned for the preservation of traditional communities, Glasser wrote about his experience of living in a remote Calabrian village in *The Net and the Quest* (1977) and a period in the north-west of Scotland resulted in *Scenes from a Highland Life* (1981). He has described how sitting for this drawing prompted within him a profound self-examination, a feeling not unlike the experience of writing his autobiographical trilogy.

Pencil on paper, 71.4 × 54.9
Bought in 1992
PG 2902

Alex Ferguson b.1941 by David Mach

Born in Govan, Alex Ferguson played football for Glasgow schools and Scotland schools before joining the amateur club Queen's Park FC in 1957. He subsequently played as a professional with several clubs, including Dunfermline Athletic and Rangers.

In 1974 Ferguson was appointed manager of East Stirlingshire and began a second, highly successful, career in club management. In 1978 he joined Aberdeen and guided 'the Dons' to three Premier Division titles, four Scottish Cup victories and one League Cup win, breaking the 'Old Firm' (Rangers and Celtic) trophy stranglehold. In 1983 Aberdeen defeated the favourites, Real Madrid, to lift the European Cup Winners' Cup.

Ferguson moved to Manchester United in 1986. His success there has been phenomenal. He twice won the League and Cup double and has recently surpassed the record of the legendary Sir Matt Busby for the number of trophies his teams have brought back to Old Trafford.

Gavin Hastings b.1962 by David Mach

Postcard and photograph
collage, 181 × 181
Bought with help from the
National Art Collections
Fund in 1997
PG 3045

Gavin Hastings retired from international rugby in 1995 having played
sixty-one matches for his country,
twenty of them as captain. He scored
over seven hundred points in official
test matches placing him second,
behind Australia's Michael Lynagh, in
the list of all-time record point
scorers.

David Mach has shown Gavin
Hastings, rugby ball tucked under his
arm, sprinting determinedly against a
background made from postcards of a
heather-covered hillside. The setting is
quintessentially Scottish, almost a
cliché of Scotland, but the colour
purple does not just call to mind a
certain aspect of Scottishness, it is also
the traditional colour of emperors, and
Gavin Hastings was for many years the
emperor of his sport.

Stephen Hendry b.1969 by David Mach

Postcard and photograph
collage, 181 × 181
Bought with help from the
National Art Collections
Fund in 1997
PG 3046

Ranked number one in the world, Hendry is probably the greatest snooker player of all time. He has won sixty-four major championships including six World Championships, six Master Championships, and five United Kingdom Championships. His prize money to date totals over £5 million.

David Mach has shown Hendry leaning over the green baize of a snooker table to pot a ball. His portrait, made from a photograph of Hendry interwoven with thousand of copies of a single postcard, has allowed the artist to exaggerate, even distort, the sportsman's body. The subject of the postcard used throughout the work is only revealed in the bottom right hand corner – the earth seen from space. The earth becomes the snooker ball – a witty reference to Hendry's mastery of his world.

Yvonne Murray b.1964 by David Mach

Postcard and photograph
collage, 181 × 181
Bought with help from the
National Art Collections
Fund in 1997
PG 3047

Edinburgh-born Murray has become one of Britain's most successful athletes of recent years. Starting as a middle-distance runner, Yvonne Murray first came to public notice when she broke the UK junior record for 3000 metres in 1982. In 1986 she was a bronze medallist at the Commonwealth Games in Edinburgh and went on to win bronze, silver and gold medals at European Championships, World Cups and the Olympic Games. During her track career, Murray has increased her running distance, winning the gold for the 10,000 metres at the 1994 Commonweath Championships and, most recently, moving on to marathons.

In Mach's collage, the larger than life photograph of Murray is interleaved with thousands of postcards of Jayne Mansfield, the glamorous Hollywood starlet who was killed in a car accident in 1967. Mach enjoyed the contrast between Yvonne, 'so kind of nice' and Mansfield, 'a sexy, busty blonde that your mother would be disturbed by if you brought her home'. The postcards show the actress (barely) clothed in leopard-skin in the alluring pose of the traditional femme-fatale, but the images are undercut, quite literally, by the dynamism inherent in Murray's slight but ecstatic tracksuit-clad figure, errupting onto the surface.

John Byrne b.1940 · *Self-portrait*

John Byrne has combined several careers – playwright, theatre designer and artist. Working for the 7:84 Theatre Company, he designed the sets for one of the most celebrated plays of the post war years, John McGrath's *The Cheviot, The Stag and the Black, Black, Oil.* In his most famous play, *The Slab Boys*, Byrne drew on his experience as a paint mixer in a Paisley carpet factory. During the 1980s Byrne wrote the cult television series *Tutti Frutti*, followed by *Your Cheatin' Heart* which used country and western music as a backdrop to a comedy of Glasgow life.

Oil on block-board,
147 × 91
Gifted by the Scottish Arts
Council in 1997
PG 3068

Robbie Coltrane b.1950 as Danny McGlone by John Byrne

Oil on board, 30 × 21.2
Bought in 1998
PG 3116

Robbie Coltrane came to national prominence with the rise of television's alternative comedy scene in the early 1980s. He starred in thirteen Comic Strip performances and received the Peter Sellers Award for comedy for his contribution to film comedy. This followed his highly successful film, *Nuns on the Run*, in which the overweight actor starred as an unlikely nun. Robbie Coltrane, who was born in Rutherglen and was a student at Glasgow School of Art, has been associated with John Byrne at several stages of his career. Coltrane was in the original production of *The Slab Boys* and its sequel *Cuttin' a Rug*. This portrait shows the actor in the character of Danny McGlone from Byrne's *Tutti Frutti*, for which Coltrane won his first nomination as best actor for a BAFTA award. As Fitz in Granada's series, *Cracker*, Coltrane has established a secure reputation as a fine straight actor.

The Citizens: Robert David MacDonald b.1929, Philip Prowse b.1937 and Giles Havergal b.1938 by *Adrian Wiszniewski*

The subjects of this portrait are the artistic directors of Glasgow's Citizens Theatre. The Citizens Company, which was founded by James Bridie in 1943, has, in recent years, become world-famous for the excellence and originality of its productions. The present Citizens Company was formed in 1970, and remains very much a living part of its local community in the Gorbals. In 1992 the company opened two studio theatres in addition to the main auditorium. Robert David MacDonald is renowned for his translations and adaptations, Philip Prowse is highly respected as a director and designer, while Giles Havergal is noted both as a

director and as a leading actor.

Adrian Wiszniewski has painted the directors in surroundings which can be interpreted either as a natural landscape or as a stage set. Stylistically, there are echoes of the paintings of the French artist Fernand Léger, whose large-scale public commissions celebrated the labour of the common man. Wiszniewski's triple portrait has been described as being 'a poetic, intelligent and beautiful work of contemporary art, as well as a subtle likeness of the three directors. It is a moving record of a vitally important part of Glasgow's post-war history – exciting and full of hope.'

Acrylic on canvas,
244 × 183
Commissioned by the
Gallery in 1995
PG 3004

Bill Forsyth b.1946 by Steven Campbell

That Sinking Feeling, a gentle comedy about a group of unemployed young people in Glasgow, was Bill Forsyth's debut feature film. Made independently, it utilised local talent and was remarkable for its style and authenticity. His second film, *Gregory's Girl*, set in Cumbernauld and made in 1980, took a similar theme of adolescence in a Scottish new town. This won universal approval for its humour and humanity. In 1983 Forsyth set *Local Hero* in the islands – 'a tale of capitalism, the environment and rabbit stew.' In 1984 he made *Comfort and Joy* about an ice-cream war. His connection with the American film industry led to

Housekeeping in 1987 and *Breaking In* in 1989. *Being Human*, made with Robin Williams in 1994, involved a partial return to Scotland, in an epic story of 'universal man', from the bronze age to modern New York.

Steven Campbell, the artist chosen for this commission, had known Forsyth for some years and sees him as 'a dark mysterious creature'. He described how he 'put Bill between town and country, by a great sweep of a motorway flyover. He often uses the Kingston Bridge at night in his films. His long arm echoes its shape and also protects his kids.'

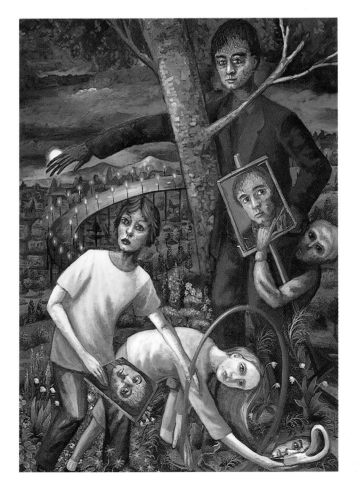

Oil on canvas, 185 × 130
Commissioned by the
Gallery in 1995
PG 2989

The Lords Cameron by Jessie Ann Matthew

This is a double portrait of two distinguished Scottish judges, 'Jock', Lord Cameron (1900–96), and his son, Kenneth John, Lord Cameron of Lochbroom (born 1931). John Cameron was born in Edinburgh. After serving in both world wars he became an advocate and a judge. In 1978 he was created a Knight of the Thistle. Kenneth John Cameron became Lord Advocate in 1984, a life peer in the same year, and a judge in 1989.

A double portrait more than doubles the challenge of an individual portrait. Besides doing justice to each of the sitters and showing something of their individual characteristics, there is a third element to consider: the relationship between them. There are signs that would tell us, if we did not know their identity, that these men are eminent – even powerful (the pin-stripes and the old school or regimental ties). They are reserved and even wary of the camera, but their close proximity to each other has been calculated by the photographer to indicate a degree of intimacy that would not be usual between colleagues, and which encourages us to note the physical resemblance. Thus, the visual clues allow us to deduce that they are father and son.

Silver gelatine photograph,
25.3 × 16.8
Bought in 1986
PGP 16.36

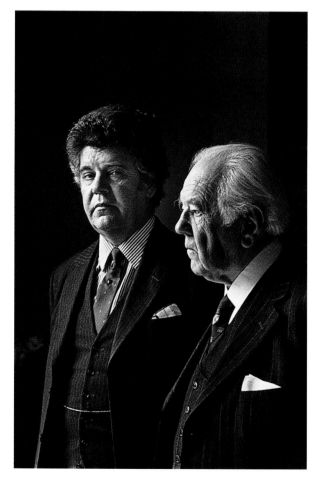

Irvine Welsh b.1958 and Duncan Maclean b.1964 by Gunnie Moberg

This photograph of two leading contemporary novelists was taken at the Edinburgh Book Festival in 1993. Maclean was born in Aberdeenshire and now lives in Orkney. Welsh has his roots in urban Scotland. He was born in Leith and was brought up in Muirhouse, an underprivileged area on the outskirts of Edinburgh. He has used his kowledge of the area's deprived and drug-ridden culture in his highly successful first novel, *Trainspotting*. The book, which is about the horror of heroin addiction, and subsequently the film based on the book, proved popular throughout the world. As the film historian David Bruce has said: 'There was no doubt that *Trainspotting* was genuinely of our culture, whether we liked it or not ... The story of Renton, Spud, Sick Boy and company living their various but related forms of hell was scarcely a celebration of Scotland in the nineties.

Politicians and tourist bosses must have been distressed at the image of the country it projected ... But it did prove the Scottish ability to make books and films of tremendous intelligence and impact about contemporary issues. That could only be a matter for great celebration.' In *Trainspotting*, and in subsequent works such as *The Acid House* and *Marabou Stork Nightmares*, Welsh has achieved his aim of giving a voice in literature to those too generally despised as an irredeemable substratum of Scottish society.

Colour photograph, 24.8 × 38
Bought in 1996
PGP 163.1

Index of Artists

Index of Sitters